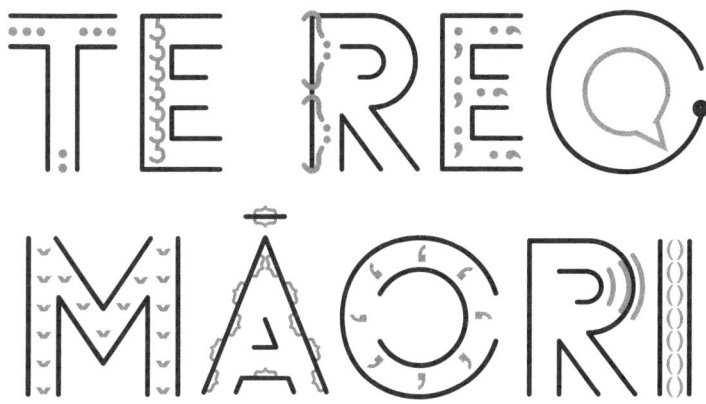

TE REO MĀORI

This book is dedicated to

Sir Tīmoti Kāretu
acknowledging his immense contribution towards
ensuring the survival of
te reo Māori as a living language.

'Time ... worships language and forgives
everyone by whom it lives ...'
— W.H. Auden

'I te tīmatanga te kupu ...'
— Ko te Rongopai ki te
Ritenga a Hoani, 1, 1

TE REO MĀORI

THE BASICS EXPLAINED

×

DAVID KĀRENA-HOLMES

Oratia

Published by Oratia Books, Oratia Media Ltd, 783 West Coast Road,
Oratia, Auckland 0604, New Zealand (www.oratia.co.nz).

ISBN 978-0-947506-69-8
Ebook ISBN 978-1-99-004204-1

First published 2020
Reprinted 2020, 2021

Printed in China

Contents

Preface

Sir Tīmoti Kāretu, to whom this book is dedicated, and who, as the first Commissioner of Māori Language contributed a foreword to this author's earlier *Māori Language: Understanding the Grammar*, has frequently stressed the need for learners of te reo Māori to acquire a sound knowledge of the principles that govern the construction of phrases and sentences in te reo.

There are considerable differences between te reo Māori and the English language in this respect. The present book — essentially a complete rewrite of the now out-of-print *Māori Language: Understanding the Grammar* — represents a further attempt by an English-speaker in an ongoing endeavour to explain at least the main differences between the two languages in as clear a manner as possible, using mostly everyday language rather than more specialised linguistic terminology.

David Kārena-Holmes
October 2019

Introduction

ONE

There are three main divisions to what is called the 'grammar' of a language: phonology (the sounds or pronunciation), morphology (the forms of words) and syntax (the ways in which words are combined to form meaningful phrases and sentences).

Correct pronunciation of *te reo Māori* must surely be acquired through practice, and more practice, in imitation of Māori speakers. In a printed book, however, it's appropriate that some comments should be made about the relationship between the spoken and written language — and this is the concern of Part 1 of this book.

Parts 2 and 3 (which form the greater part of the book) are concerned almost entirely with syntax. The word 'syntax' however is often considered interchangeable with 'grammar' — and it is this broader and more familiar term that is used throughout. The contents of part 2 might be described as preparatory material, outlining principles that are the basis for the more comprehensive and detailed coverage in part 3, which is the main section of the book.

Descriptions of grammar provide one kind of bridge between the languages for users of English to gain some appreciation of the subtlety and beauty of expression manifested not only in the sounds but also in the structure of phrases and sentences in *te reo Māori*.

Something far more important than only what might be called

'aesthetic appreciation' is involved here. Dr Karena Kelly, in her essay 'Iti te Kupu, Nui te Kōrero: The Study of the Little Details that Make the Māori Language Māori', clearly articulates the profound concern that if not enough attention is given to the finer points of the grammar there is a real risk of *te reo Māori* becoming:

> *more and more like a clone of English, a mere hybridised*
> *shadow of the vibrant language we call te reo rangatira*
> *(the chiefly language).*[1]

This means that what is at stake is nothing less than a unique 'world view'. A language and its grammatical structures connect with the very roots of our being, influence how we perceive the world and play a part in determining our behaviour. Language is inseparable from these things. The structure of a phrase or sentence, it could be said, is a manifestation of the structure of thought.

Understanding the grammar, then, as Scotty Morrison has put it bluntly in his *The Raupō Phrasebook of Modern Māori*, 'eventually becomes vital to proficiency in te reo.'

TWO

The different ways in which phrases and sentences are constructed in *te reo Māori* may be described in English, but this certainly does not mean that the so-called traditional English grammar is always appropriate or applicable to *te reo*.

This has long been recognised. As Robert Maunsell expressed in the preface to his 1842 *Grammar of the New Zealand Language*:

> *Upon this only would [I] insist, in reply to those who*
> *would bind [me] down to the model of some of the*
> *European grammars, that Māori, like Hebrew, is altogether*
> *different from those languages in structure …*

9

To be sure, in *te reo* words are used in groups that may be called phrases and sentences, as they are in English. Also, there are words that may, for instance, be said to function as nouns, verbs and prepositions. But that, without too much exaggeration, is about where the similarity between the languages ends.

Te reo Māori, however, is not more complicated than English. In fact, when considered on its own terms *te reo* is, in several ways, simpler, and frequently more logical, grammatically, than English.

In 1948 the Danish historian of religion, Jörgen Prytz-Johansen, published a finely-articulated study of some aspects of *te reo* in his *Character and Structure of the Action in Maori*; but not until 1969 — nearly 150 years after the 1820 publication of the first substantial attempt to explain the grammar of *te reo Māori* to speakers of English (the Church Missionary Society's *A Grammar and Vocabulary of the Language of New Zealand*) — was a grammar fully appropriate to *te reo* 'on its own terms' finally made widely available with the first edition of Bruce Biggs' *Let's Learn Maori*.

In Section 16 of his book Bruce Biggs explains:

> *In* Let's Learn Maori *an entirely different grammatical theory is used and a more simplified system of classification results. All words are divided into two classes, bases and particles. The particles … are the grammatical words; they are few in number … All other words are bases.*

The system of classification outlined in *Let's Learn Maori* (hereafter *LLM*) provides for a much clearer and simpler way for speakers of English to understand the construction of phrases and sentences in *te reo Māori* than does a kind of 'patch and mend' approach using traditional English grammar.

THREE

Since the first edition of *LLM* in 1969, much has happened. Many new books have appeared, including two major grammar books: Winifred Bauer's *The Reed Reference Grammar of Māori* in 1997 (a more accessible version of her *Maori* of 1993) and Ray Harlow's *A Māori Reference Grammar* (2001). Both publications expand on Professor Biggs' work and both are considerably more comprehensive than *LLM*.

The insights provided by Bauer, Harlow and other scholars are now being incorporated into more recent publications, such as John Moorfield's two-way dictionary, *Te Aka* (first edition 2005), and the magnificent monolingual dictionary published by Raupō in conjunction with Te Taura Whiri i te Reo Māori (The Māori Language Commission): *He Pātaka Kupu — te kai a te rangatira* (*A Storehouse of Words — the food of a chief*, 2008).

Published entirely in *te **reo Māori**, He Pātaka Kupu* may appear daunting to the second-language learner approaching it for the first time. But it has rightly been described as 'a significant milestone in the history of the Māori language'. Confidence in accessing this resource might be seen as a goal to which learners could aspire.

Within the same period technological developments have also provided the online medium for several excellent learning programs in which grammatical explanations are given, such as *Kupu o te Rā*.

Thus, the 'new' grammar advocated in *LLM*, with some modifications, is being progressively introduced. But there is still quite a long way to go before the essential simplicity of this grammar finds the widespread general acceptance it merits.

FOUR

In *Te Reo Māori: the Basics Explained,* no prior knowledge of grammar is assumed, not even of elementary terminology. The main purpose is to provide clear and simple explanations of the most significant differences between te reo Māori and the English language, primarily by reference to the 'new' grammar developed by Bruce Biggs in the 1960s.

From this point onwards, each key term, usually when first introduced (and intermittently elsewhere) is printed in SMALL CAPITALS. The meaning, and/or function of each of these terms, even if not explicitly defined, should be clear from the context in which it is used. Certain other typographic conventions are employed so that the constructions of the Māori PHRASES and SENTENCES should be visually as self-explanatory as possible. These conventions are as follows.

In order that Māori text should be readily distinguishable from English, all Māori words hereafter (with the single exception of the word 'Māori' when it is used in the English text) are in italic script. The only occasions where English words are italicised are for some quotations and (following standard practice) with titles of books.

In most of the Māori sentences presented as examples the phrases are separated one from the other. Directly beneath each phrase is given a literal translation into English of that particular phrase. Then (but only when considered necessary) beneath the literal translation, is given a rendering of the overall meaning of the sentence in idiomatic English (in quotation marks and enclosed in brackets). The following examples should make these conventions clear:

*E **haere** mai ana*   *ngā **manuhiri.***

are moving this way   the visitors

('The visitors are coming.')

*E **haere** ana*	*au*	*ki te **whare**.*
am moving	I	to the house.

('I am going to the house.')

A further convention followed (also illustrated in the above examples) is that certain words in the Māori phrases are shown in **bold print**. These are the BASE WORDS (in some books simply called BASES). The other words are collectively called PARTICLES.

The intention in distinguishing BASE WORDS by bold print in this manner is to make the construction of phrases more visually obvious. However, because it turns out that there are, in fact, some words in te reo which don't exactly fit into one or other of the two categories of BASE WORDS or PARTICLES, this convention (BASE WORDS in bold print) does involve compromise in some cases. More specific details are provided in the relevant sections in chapters 2, 4 and 13.

---

1. In Higgins, Rawinia,; Rewi, Poia and Olsen-Reeder, Vincent (eds.), *The Value of the Māori Language/Te Hua o te Reo Māori*. Huia Publishers, Wellington, 2014, p. 26.

PART 1

The written form of the sounds of te reo Māori

1
Pronunciation and the written form of te reo Māori

Attempts to produce a written form for *te reo* began in the late eighteenth century, and some early efforts produced what appear, today, as rather bizarre results. Although suggestions for modification are still put forward from time to time, the now generally approved standard form of the alphabet for written Māori, consists of the following 15 symbols:

FIVE VOWEL LETTERS

a e i o u

EIGHT SINGLE CONSONANT LETTERS

h k m n p r t w

TWO DIGRAPH CONSONANTS

ng wh

This is one of the shortest and simplest of alphabets among the world's languages.

In Kai Tahu dialect a *k* often replaces the *ng*, thus reducing the list to 14 symbols. In other dialects fewer than the 15 symbols are employed, and in some cases (such as the Waitaha/Rapuvai use of '*g*' and '*v*') speakers use written symbols additional to those in the alphabet above.

One advantage of the fact that a written form for *te reo Māori* has been developed in this manner is that there is consistency between spelling and pronunciation. This means that there is none of the confusion that exists in English where, for instance, any vowel might have a different sound in one word to that which it has in another, for example, the vowel 'o' in the words 'to' and 'go'. In English, the letters 'ow' have quite different pronunciation in the words 'low' and 'how'; and (a notorious example) the letters 'ough' may represent any one of at least seven sounds ('bough', 'bought', 'cough', 'enough', 'through', 'thorough', 'though').

There are, however, several regional variations in the pronunciation of *te reo* to be noted, particularly in relation to words which, in standard written form, make use of either of the two digraphs *ng* and *wh*.

In some cases the difference in pronunciation is made clear by the spelling of the word (for example, *tanata, takata, tagata* are all variations of, and mean the same as, *tangata* — 'person'). Brief comments about these variations are found below, under the section on the consonants.

Some remnants of early attempts at writing te **reo** are embedded in place names on maps. The letter *l*, for instance, used in the south in some cases instead of the now standard *r*, survives in the place names **Waihola, Wangaloa** and **Kilmog** (the last being a local variation of the word for which the standard spelling is *kirimoko*).

THE SOUNDS IN *TE REO MĀORI*

The five letters *a, e, i, o* and *u* serve to represent the five vowel sounds of *te reo*. It's interesting to note that when the English names of these letters are spoken none of them has the sound they represent in written Māori.

The vowel sounds in Māori are all pure vowel sounds. A pure vowel sound is a sound that can be prolonged indefinitely without alteration. Thus:

> Aaaaaaaaaa … (as 'a' in the English word 'father').

The spoken sound of the English name of the letter 'a', by contrast, is not a single, pure vowel sound, but a DIPHTHONG (double vowel sound), beginning with one sound, which then mutates into another. An approximation of this sound may be written in Māori as *ei*. The sounds of the English names of the letters 'i', 'o' and 'u' are also diphthongs — and may be written in Māori as *ai, ou* and *iu* respectively. The sound of the English name of the letter 'e' is represented in Māori by a lengthened *i*.

The vowel sounds of *te reo* may be either short or long, and many words with quite different meanings are distinguished one from another solely by the length of a vowel sound. The approved manner of indicating long vowel sounds, in print, is placing a MACRON above the letter, thus: *ā, ē, ī, ō, ū*. (with the letter *i* the macron replaces the dot).

The sounds may be indicated by comparison to sounds in English words, as follows:

LONG SOUNDS	SHORT SOUNDS
ā – as 'a' in 'f<u>a</u>ther'	*a* – as 'a' in '<u>a</u>bout'
ē – as 'ea' in 'w<u>ea</u>r'	*e* – as 'e' in 'b<u>e</u>t'
ī – as 'i' in 'mach<u>i</u>ne'	*i* – as 'i' in '<u>i</u>gloo'
ō – as 'oa' in 'b<u>oa</u>rd'	*o* – as 'o' in 'rep<u>o</u>rt'
ū – as 'oo' in 'sp<u>oo</u>n'	*u* – as 'u' in 'p<u>u</u>t'

*Te **reo Māori*** is a language full of vowel sounds. No two
consonants (disregarding the digraphs) ever occur consecutively.
But, in a single word up to five vowels may do so — as in the
word *aeaea* ('to be gasping or panting'). Peter J. Keegan (on
his website, *He Kōrero mō Te reo Māori*) has pointed out that
even complete sentences may occur without the use of a single
consonant, for example, *I auau ia*. ('He, or she, barked.')

THE SYLLABLES

A SYLLABLE in Māori may consist of a single vowel or a diphthong,
or of a consonant followed by a single vowel or a diphthong. A
chart of syllables is frequently reproduced as follows.

a	*e*	*i*	*o*	*u*
ha	*he*	*hi*	*ho*	*hu*
ka	*ke*	*ki*	*ko*	*ku*
ma	*me*	*mi*	*mo*	*mu*
na	*ne*	*ni*	*no*	*nu*
nga	*nge*	*ngi*	*ngo*	*ngu*
pa	*pe*	*pi*	*po*	*pu*
ra	*re*	*ri*	*ro*	*ru*
ta	*te*	*ti*	*to*	*tu*
wa	*we*	*wi*	*wo*	*wu*
wha	*whe*	*whi*	*who*	*whu*

It has sometimes been asserted that since vowels may be either long or short, such a chart gives a complete list of 110 possible syllables in te **reo** (although the syllables *wo, wō, wu, wū, who, whō, whu* and *whū* apparently did not occur in 'classical' Māori — that is, *te reo Māori* as it was prior to the arrival of Europeans). To this scheme, however, must be added those pairs of vowels that form single syllables (diphthongs). All possible pairs of vowels, with the exception of the vowel-pair *uo*, are present in Māori, as follows:

ae, ai, ao, au, ea, ei, eo, eu, ia, ie, io, iu, oa, oe, oi, ou, ua, ue, ui

Many of these vowel-pairs are spoken as two syllables, each vowel being pronounced as a single syllable, thus: *i-a, i-e, u-i* and so on.

But ten at least are considered to form single-syllable diphthongs. These are the pairs:

ae, ai, ao, au, ei, eu, iu, oi, oe, ou

Thus, the word *haere*, for instance, consists of only two syllables: *hae-re*.

When these ten diphthongs are matched with consonants in a chart like that above, the list of syllables available in Māori is increased to 220.

This list can be further extended when 'long diphthongs' (those diphthongs in which one of the vowels is lengthened) are added — but the list of possible syllables is still far short of the thousands of syllables possible in English.

In the pronunciation of vowel-pairs, the presence of both vowels should be clearly indicated. This applies even when the two vowels of a pair 'blend' smoothly to form a diphthong.

The conclusion here is that words such as *kai* ('to eat' or 'food'), *pai* ('to be good' or 'goodness') and *moe* ('to sleep' or 'to marry') are single-syllable words, while words such as *hoa* ('friend') and *kia* are of two syllables.

The fact that some pairs of vowels form diphthongs while other pairs remain as two syllables has large implications in relation to pronunciation.

For instance, in the greeting *Kia ora!* each word, individually, is of two syllables, but the vowel pair *a* + *o* forms a single-syllable diphthong (even when it bridges two words). This means that the expression as a whole should not be pronounced in four syllables as: *Ki-a-o-ra!*, but in three, as: *Ki-ao-ra!* Similarly, the word *uaua* ('to be difficult') is not pronounced as *u-a-u-a*, but as *u-au-a*.

There are other situations, however, where two adjacent vowels that can form a diphthong are pronounced separately. This occurs particularly when a prefix is added to a word — as in the use of the prefixes *whaka-* and *tua-*.

For instance, the words for 'cardinal' numbers: *tahi* ('one'), *rua* ('two'), *toru* ('three') and so on, are converted to 'ordinal' forms by using the prefix tua-. Thus, *tuatahi* ('first'), *tuarua* ('second'), *tuatoru* ('third') and so on. But the *a* of *tua-* does not quite blend into a diphthong with either the *o* of *ono* ('six') or the *i* of *iwa* ('nine'). The words *tuaono* ('sixth') and *tuaiwa* ('ninth') are both pronounced with four syllables. Such differences are slight, vary from speaker to speaker, and might legitimately be disputed.

THE CONSONANTS

The consonants *h, k, m, n, p, t,* and *w* are used for *te reo Māori* much as they are used in English. Remarks here will be confined to the use of the other three consonants, *ng, r* and *wh*.

The *ng* sound does occur in English — in the word 'singer' for instance — but not at the beginning of words. In English, if we break the word 'singer' into syllables it would normally be in the form 'sing-er'. Similarly with 'hang-ar'.

In Māori, on the other hand, every syllable is considered to end in a vowel, and a word such as *hinga* ('to be fallen') is shown in syllables as *hi-nga*. The *ng* can thus be practiced simply by breaking the English word 'singer' into syllables in the manner in which Māori words are broken, as: 'si-nger'.

In some regions the *ng* sound may be replaced by, variously, *n*, *k* or *g*.

The *r* sound should not be 'rolled', but 'tapped'. Early English attempts at writing words that employed this sound included use (in the north) of *d* and (in the south) of *l*.

A rolled *r* is so disliked that Quinton Hita, in his *Q's Course in Māori*, goes to the length of having the 'tutor' character in the book advise his pupil that if he is unable to avoid rolling the *r*, he should settle for pronouncing it as *l*!

The *wh* is widely accepted as representing the sound for which 'f' is used in other languages. The *wh* was the last symbol to be added to the alphabet. In the 1820 Church Missionary Society *Grammar and Vocabulary of the Language of New Zealand*, for instance, the words that are normally written now as *whare* and *whanau* are spelt as *Wáre* and *Wánau* (which still represent well the current pronunciation of some speakers).

The *wh* doesn't appear in the Treaty of Waitangi. On that document the word for 'agreement' (for instance) appears as *wakaaetanga*. This word now (in standard form) is written *whakaaetanga*. Twelve years after the 1840 treaty the *wh* is found in the 2nd edition of William Williams' Māori dictionary (*A dictionary of the New Zealand language, and a concise grammar, to which is added a selection of colloquial sentences*, 1852).

Several common words have variant, dialect spellings using *h* and *wh*. Examples are the words *hea?*/*whea?* ('where?'), *pōhiri*/*pōwhiri* ('to beckon or welcome'; or the ceremony of welcoming visitors) and *kōhatu*/*kōwhatu* ('stone').

A relatively recent dispute over the correct spelling of the name of a river and a city (**W(h)anganui**) indicates that issues around the use of *wh* remain ongoing. Ray Harlow is firmly of the opinion that, nowadays, wherever the spelling uses *wh*, the 'most usual' pronunciation is as an 'f'.

THE PLACING OF STRESS

Te reo Māori is not a heavily stressed language, but certainly, in the rhythms of speech some components of phrases carry more stress than others.

The principles seem to be, firstly, that the main stress in a phrase will occur on the base word (the first if there is more than one in the nucleus of the phrase). Within that word the stress should be on the first long vowel, if there is one; and if there is not a long vowel, then on the first diphthong, if there is one; and if there is no long vowel or diphthong, then on the first syllable. Particles, in most situations, do not usually carry a stress.

The best way of picking up the stress-rhythms of the language is obviously, as stated at the beginning of this chapter, by listening to good fluent speakers.

FURTHER COMPARISONS WITH ENGLISH

In English, the spelling of a word often provides little guidance to its sound. How, for instance, can someone unfamiliar with English be expected to recognise that the words 'to' and 'go' have different vowel sounds? Or that the words 'to', 'too' and 'two' all sound the same — and all have the same vowel sound as 'through'? Or that the 'o' of 'go', despite being a single letter, actually represents a diphthong or double vowel sound?

Because of these variations between sound and spelling, it is usual in dictionaries of English that a guide to the pronunciation of each word is given in the form of a 'phonetic transcription'.

This feature of a dictionary is not needed for Māori words because the syllables used for *te reo* are, in themselves, a phonetic system — with each syllable representing a specific sound. (The only notable exceptions to this rule would seem to be those of the variations, mentioned earlier, in relation to the pronunciation of the *ng* and *wh* digraphs, and perhaps that of the syllables beginning with *r*.)

TRANSLITERATIONS

There are many words used in *te reo* as it is spoken today that have been adopted from other languages, mostly from English. In the adoption of a word the best approximation of the sound of the original is sought, using exclusively the sound system of *te reo*.

This means that for the written form of these 'transliterations' only the syllables available to te **reo** are used — but this includes the eight syllables *wo, wō, wu, wū, who, whō, whu* and *whū*, which apparently have not been found in classical Māori.

It would be difficult, most likely impossible, to establish a complete system of 'rules' for transliteration because of the many compromises that are unavoidable. With English, this is due to the great range of vowel sounds in the language, and to the fact that English frequently uses sequences of two or more consecutive consonants (something that does not occur in *te reo*).

Although certain ways of spelling common words are undoubtedly now regarded as 'standard', because transliterations are approximations only, variant forms are quite common, and it can hardly be insisted that any particular spelling of a transliteration must be considered the only 'correct' one.

A few widely followed principles may, however, be noted. Some of the vowel sounds have already been mentioned above. Consonants in the English alphabet that are not used in the alphabet of te **reo** are commonly transliterated as follows.

- The hard 'c' of English is conveniently replaced by the *k* of *te reo*, while the soft 'c', 'ch', 'j', 's' 'sh','x' and 'z' may all be transliterated by Māori *h*. Both 'd' and 'l' of English are replaced by *r* in *te reo*; while English 'g' is normally replaced by *k* (although, as already mentioned, some speakers in the south actually use a '*g*' in their spelling).
- Some southern speakers also use a *v* in spelling (for example, the tribal name **Rapuvai**) but in most dialects English 'v' is replaced by Māori *w* (as in **Kuini Wikitoria**, which also shows *Ku* substituting for English 'Qu').
- The English 'b' normally becomes *p* in *te reo*. English 'f' (and 'ph') in some instances, are rendered by Māori *p*, for example, **Pepuere** ('February') and ***poropiti*** ('prophet'). This is interesting in relation to the issues surrounding the use of the Māori *wh*. The spelling ***porowhiti*** (for 'prophet') could hardly be considered absolutely wrong. English 'f' is transliterated by Māori *wh* in many other words, for example, ***whutupaoro*** ('football').

Certainly, there are many anomalies. The 'a' in the English word 'station', for instance, has the same sound as the 'a' in 'plate', but the representation in *te reo* differs, one from the other:

'station' — ***teihana***; 'plate' — ***pereti***.

The pronunciation, and thus the spelling of the word ***pereti*** presumably results from the attempt to suggest the adjoining consonants 'pl' of the English word.

Personal names offer a great range of examples of transliterations, for example:

Anaru ('Andrew'); *Karoraina* ('Caroline'), *Raniera* ('Daniel'); *Irihāpeti* ('Elizabeth'); *Hēmi* ('James')

Where an English word ends with a consonant a vowel must be added in the transliteration (all syllables in *te reo Māori* end in a vowel). It would seem that any of the five short vowels of *te reo* might be used to fill this position, for example:

teihana; ('station'); *pene* ('pen'); *hipi* ('sheep'); *kōti* ('court' of law); *paoro* or *pōro* ('ball'); *kapu* ('cup')

Note A great number of transliterations have been introduced into classical or 'pure' *te reo Māori* over the past two centuries. A glance through the pages of the *He Pātaka Kupu* reveals many entries described as originating from a *reo kē* ('other language'). It should be emphasised, though, that where an original Māori word is available for a particular purpose it should be given preference over a transliteration, for example, the word *whaea* ('mother') is to be preferred to *mama*.

PART 2

Discovering the new grammar

2
Sentences, phrases, words

A SENTENCE has been defined as a word or a set of words that forms a complete statement, question, exclamation or command. This definition applies to *te reo Māori* just as much as it does to English. Thus, the single-word command **Whakarongo**! ('Listen!') is a complete sentence.

More often sentences are composed of several words, which may be grouped in one or more PHRASES. In the *Oxford Dictionary* a PHRASE is defined as 'a small group of words standing together as a conceptual unit.' But a phrase **may** consist of a single word.

A phrase **may** form a complete statement (and therefore **may** stand as a complete sentence), as with **Whakarongo**!, or as with the courteous phrase of welcome:

Haere *mai!*
move hither
('Come here!')

Commonly, a sentence consists of two or more linked phrases (in the examples in this book phrases are separated, one from the other, by a large space):

E *haere* ana	*au*	ki te *whare*.
moving	I	to the house

('I am going to the house.')

In this sentence, the combination of the first two phrases — *E haere ana au* ('I am going') — could stand on its own as a complete sentence, but none of the phrases, individually, constitutes a complete sentence. Some significant points are illustrated in the above example.

In the Māori sentence the VERB PHRASE — *E haere ana* ('am going') — comes first in the sequence of phrases, while the SUBJECT PHRASE — *au* — occupies the second position. This is the reverse of the most common sequence of phrases in English and is one of the major differences between English and *te reo Māori*. The common pattern for simple sentences in *te reo* (note that there are many exceptions) is with the subject phrase in the second position of the phrase sequence.

In linguistic terms, while English belongs in a group of languages characterised as **S**ubject-**V**erb-**O**bject sequence (SVO), *te reo Māori* belongs in the group of **V**erb-**S**ubject-**O**bject (VSO) sequence languages.

Although *te reo* as a VSO language belongs to one of the largest language **groups** in the world, because major languages — Mandarin, Spanish, English — are of the SVO type, the total number of speakers of SVO languages vastly exceeds the number of VSO language speakers.

Another quite different point is that **sometimes** (but **only** sometimes), as is the case with the third phrase — *ki te whare* ('to the house') — the patterns of phrases in *te reo* have word-for-word parallels in English translation.

Far more frequently, as is the case with the first phrase — *E haere ana* ('am going') — they are not so paralleled. This is a VERB PHRASE in which the base word — *haere* — is used as a verb meaning 'to move' ('go' or 'come', but usually 'go' unless it is followed by the DIRECTION PARTICLE *mai*). But there are no English words to translate the Māori words *E ... ana*.

The words *E ... ana* are VERB PARTICLES that mark the verb phrase as being in a 'continuous' TENSE. Although the translation above has been given as 'am going', it should be noted that this 'tense' may be used when referring to the past, present or future — just as in English one might say, 'I am going out tomorrow.' The phrase *E **haere** ana* might translate as 'am, are, is, was, were or will be, going' according to context.

It might be noted here that there is also a very common dialectal alternative that uses the particles *kei te* (or *kai te*) preceding the base word to indicate the 'continuous' tense. *Kei te **haere** ...* may mean the same as *E **haere** ana ...* (for further information see chapters 6 and 12).

Rarely, if ever, does a Māori sentence of any great length have exactly the same phrase order, or word order, as that of its appropriate English translation. This means that the construction of phrases and the composition of sentences in Māori, while they can be compared and contrasted with English constructions, must be understood and appreciated on their own terms, independently from the grammar of English.

Taking the time to understand thoroughly, from the outset, exactly how even such a simple sentence as the above example is constructed can be an important initial step in understanding how phrases and sentences of several different types are composed in *te **reo** Māori*.

PHRASES ARE COMPOSED OF WORDS

The terms BASE WORDS and PARTICLES have already been introduced. BASE WORDS — identifiable in the Māori text in this book by being printed in bold italic — are those words that have what may be called real meaning. That is, they have a meaning we understand as referring to things, actions, events and so on, which exist in the world of our experiences (including objects, places, people and the things they do, and even thoughts, wishes and emotions in the mind).

Words such as *haere* ('to move'), *au* and its free variant *ahau* (both signifying 'I' or 'me'), and *whare* ('house' or 'building') are examples of BASE WORDS.

Here, again, is the sentence from above:

E *haere ana*	*au*	*ki te **whare**.*
moving	I	to the house
('I am going to the house.')		

It might seem that most of the meaning of this sentence could be well enough, if perhaps clumsily, conveyed by the base words alone:

… *haere* …	*au* …	*whare.*
move (or go)	I	house

But the precise meaning of any phrase or sentence as a whole is determined by the other words, the little supporting words collectively called PARTICLES, which combine with the base words to make fluent and coherent phrases and sentences.

PARTICLES cannot be said to have translatable meaning in the same way that base words have meaning. Rather, they have structural functions in the forming of phrases and sentences. They are items of language that do not refer to things in the world in the way that base words do. Their frame of reference is entirely within their use in language.

If a sentence is likened to a stone wall, then the base words could be said to represent the stones, while the particles represent the mortar or cement that binds the stones together into a coherent, meaningful whole.

A phrase in *te reo Māori* is formed around a 'stone' or 'nucleus' of one or more base words. One or two particles (normally never more than two) may precede the nucleus of a phrase. The COMMON NOUN *whare* is the nucleus of the following phrases:

... *te whare* ... ('the house')
... *ki te whare* ... ('to the house')

One or more particles (sometimes as many as four or five) may follow the nucleus. The ACTION VERB *haere* is the nucleus of these two phrases:

Haere *mai!* ('Come here!')
E **haere** *mai ana* ... ('Coming here ...')

In many phrases there may be particles in both positions (as in the example above, *E* **haere** *mai ana* ...).

The particles may therefore be considered in two categories: those that normally **precede** the nucleus of the phrase, and those that normally **follow** the nucleus. Within each of these two broad categories the particles may be classified into several specific groups. From chapter 11 onwards the focus of this book is on clarifying the functions of particles.

Māori words such as *te* (often to be translated as 'the' when the reference is to one thing only), *ngā* ('the' — for more than one thing) and *ki* (often signifying the same as the English words 'to' or 'towards' but there are several other uses) are examples of PARTICLES.

Again, **almost all** of the words in *te reo Māori* (but not quite all) may be identified as belonging to one or other of these **two primary categories**:

BASE WORDS   PARTICLES

There are thousands of BASE WORDS in *te reo Māori,* and new words are more or less continuously being added to the list. It is the **meaning** of each, **as well as how each is functioning in a given phrase**, which should be understood.

3
Verb phrases and noun phrases

Here, again, is a sentence from the previous chapter:

*E **haere** ana*	*au*	*ki te **whare**.*
moving	I	to the house

('I am going to the house.')

This sentence shows examples of the two types of phrase in *te reo Māori*: VERB PHRASE and NOUN PHRASE.

The first phrase — *E **haere** ana* — is marked as a verb phrase by the fact that the base word is enclosed by the VERB PARTICLES *E ... ana*, which signify that the verb is in the 'continuous' tense. The other two phrases (*au* and *ki te **whare***) are both NOUN PHRASES.

The essential feature of a phrase in Māori, whether it is a noun phrase or a verb phrase, is a **nucleus**. A **nucleus** is composed (almost always) of **one or more** base words.

Sometimes the nucleus of a phrase consists simply of a single base word standing on its own, as with *Whakarongo!* ('Listen!'). More often, the base word nucleus is preceded and/or followed by one or more particles, as in the phrases *E **haere** ana* ... and ... *ki te **whare***.

Here is a more extended sentence, taken from the Māori version of the biblical *The Book of Revelation*, chapter 22):

Ka whakakitea mai	*e ia*	*ki ahau*
shown	by him	to me

he awa wai ora	*pīata tonu*	*me te karāihe*
a river water life	clear very	as the crystal

e puta mai ana	*i te torōna*	*o te Atua.*
emerging	from the throne	of the God.

('He showed me a river of the water of life, clear as crystal, emerging from the throne of God.')

This example illustrates that in some phrases *te reo* requires particles where English doesn't have any words — as in *e puta mai ana* ('emerging').

In other phrases there are no words in *te reo* corresponding to some of the words in English, for example, *he awa wai ora*, where there are only four words (while there are seven words in 'a river of the water of life').

English meanings can be given to all the base words, but only some of the particles need be translated into English, and others simply don't have any English translation.

The preceding example illustrates most of the patterns of phrases in *te reo*.

- A phrase in *te reo* always has a 'nucleus' of at least one base word;
- or more than one base word, for example:

he awa wai ora

- often with either one or two particles before the nucleus (normally **never more than two** particles precede the nucleus), for example:

  e ia and *me te karāihe*

- or one or more particles following the nucleus, for example:

  pīata tonu and *e puta mai ana*

- or with one or more particles both preceding and following the nucleus, for example:

  Ka whakakitea mai and *e puta mai ana.*

A further type of phrase, not represented above, consists of a base word alone, without any particles. An example, from the previous chapter, is: **Whakarongo!**

PHRASES AND THEIR HEAD WORDS

In *te reo Māori* phrases belong in one or the other of two main groups:

NOUN PHRASES   VERB PHRASES

In a noun phrase the HEAD WORD — the main base word in the phrase (and usually the first if there is more than one) — is a base word functioning as a noun.

Thus, *awa* ('river') is the head word in the noun phrase *he awa wai ora* ('a river of life-giving water').

In a verb phrase the HEAD WORD is a base word functioning as a verb.

Thus, **puta** is the HEAD WORD in the verb phrase *e **puta** mai ana* ('emerging').

The sentence from *The Book of Revelation* consists of nine phrases, three are verb phrases and six are noun phrases. The verb phrases are:

*Ka **whakakitea** mai* ('shown hither'), ***pīata** tonu* ('very clear') and *e **puta** mai ana* ('emerging hither').

Readers familiar with the concept of a verb as a 'doing word', and following the above English translations, should have no trouble recognising the phrases *Ka **whakakitea** mai* and e **puta** *mai* ana as verb phrases — since both these phrases refer to actions or 'things being **done**'.

Not quite so obvious, perhaps, is why the phrase ***pīata** tonu* should also be regarded as a verb phrase. The Māori base word ***pīata*** is translated here by the English ADJECTIVE (descriptive word) 'clear'. (The particle *tonu* simply intensifies the meaning.)

Why then should the Māori phrase ***pīata** tonu* be identified as a VERB PHRASE rather than as an 'adjectival phrase'? To some readers this question may seem of little consequence — but it actually brings attention to one of the most significant differences of all between *te **reo** Māori* and English.

This difference consists in the fact that while in English the main verbs are 'doing words', verbs in *te **reo** Māori* may be **either** '**doing words**' or '**being words**'.

Verb phrases in *te **reo*** are of two main types: those that denote **action** and those that denote **state** — or, it could be said, those identified as PHRASES OF DOING and those identified as PHRASES OF BEING. In a SENTENCE in *te **reo*** such as:

*Ka **pai** te **mahi** nei.*

it would not be wrong to translate the first phrase as 'is good', but it is incorrect to suggest that the Māori particle *ka* might somehow correspond to the English linking word 'is'. The particle *ka* does not have any equivalent in English. This is easily demonstrated by comparing the above sentence in which the verb phrase denotes a **state**, with another Māori sentence in which the verb phrase denotes an **action**:

Ka *pai*   te *mahi nei.*

is good   the work here

('This work is good.')

Ka *oma*   te **kurī**.

Runs   the dog

('The dog runs.')

It might be added that while the phrase *ka pai* might be translated in one context as 'is good', the translation, in another context, might be 'am good', 'are good' or even 'will be good'.

The particle *ka* is one of the verb particles, that is, one of those particles that signify that the base word following it is functioning as a verb (which may denote an **action** or a **state**).

Indeed, it could be given as a definition of verb that **any word** that follows the particle *ka* **directly** is functioning as a verb. The phrase *ka pai* is a verb phrase meaning '**in a good state**'.

Because this particular difference between English verbs and those of *te reo* Māori is so significant, much of the next chapter is given over to fuller consideration of exactly how the classes of base words in *te reo* differ from those of English.

4
Classification
of words

If the term BASE WORD is applied to English it could be taken to refer to verbs, nouns, adjectives and at least some adverbs — but the words in these classes are by no means exactly paralleled in *te reo Māori*.

VERBS

In discussing the grammar of English it is common practice to state that a verb is a 'doing word'. This concept of a verb as simply a 'doing word' is widespread. The 5th edition of *New Zealand School Oxford Dictionary*, for instance, defines VERB as: 'a word that shows what a person or thing is doing.' This definition is **quite inadequate** for *te reo Māori*.

Describing a VERB, in English, as a 'doing word' is perhaps acceptable only because **almost all verbs in English** are words that denote some sort of action. But in English there are other types of verb, such as what is sometimes called the 'copula' or 'linking verb', the verb 'to be'.

Descriptive sentences are frequently composed in English using a 'part' of this verb (such as 'am', 'are', 'is', 'were' or 'was') followed by the type of descriptive word that is known as an adjective, for example, 'good':

This talk	is	good.
These people	are	good.

Descriptive sentences may also be formed by using a part of the verb 'to be' followed by a word that is called the PAST PARTICIPLE of a verb, for example, 'finished':

The work	is	finished.

The fact that that there is no equivalent of the English verb 'to be' in *te reo Māori* means that sentences with the same meaning as the English examples given are made in a quite different way in *te reo*. They are made with what are termed STATIVE VERBS (or just STATIVES). These are verbs that refer to a 'state' rather than an action.

There are many BASE WORDS in *te reo* that function as VERBS — but it would be wrong to think of these, collectively, as 'doing words'. In fact, a more correct definition of VERB, in broader linguistic terms, is as 'a word that denotes an **action, or** a **state**'. Some dictionaries do, in fact, define a VERB as a word denoting **'doing' or 'being'**.

In *te reo Māori*, certainly, there are many BASE WORDS that appear in VERB PHRASES and that denote some form of action or 'doing' — and that might therefore, be called ACTION VERBS (for example, *haere, puta, whakarongo*). In contrast to English, there are in *te reo* also many BASE WORDS used in VERB PHRASES that do not denote action. Instead, they denote a **state** of 'being'.

The Māori word *pai* commonly functions as a STATIVE VERB, used to describe something as 'being in a good state':

> Ka *pai*   *tēnei* **kōrero**.
>
> is good   this talk.
>
> ('This talk is good.')

> Kua **mutu**   *te mahi*.
>
> is finished   the work
>
> ('The work is finished.')

In *te reo* there is no equivalent of the English linking verb 'to be'. Instead, there are two main classes of verb:

ACTION VERBS	STATIVE VERBS
EXAMPLES	EXAMPLES
haere ('to go')	*pai* ('to be good')
kōrero ('to speak')	*ora* ('to be well')
mahi ('to work')	*mutu* ('to be finished')
waiata ('to sing')	*pakaru* ('to be broken')
noho ('to sit or stay')	*whero* ('to be red')

Many words from both these classes may be used also as COMMON NOUNS. For instance, in some contexts *kōrero* may denote 'speech'; *waiata* may denote 'song'; *pai* may signify 'goodness'). Separate chapters are given to ACTION VERBS and STATIVE VERBS in Part 3 of this book.

Note It's true also that many words from these classes — particularly stative verbs such as *pai* — may be used to 'qualify' a noun — just as adjectives are in English — and further discussion on this point follows in the last section of this chapter.

NOUNS

The other primary category of BASE WORD is NOUNS.

NOUNS give names to things. They are 'naming' words. In English NOUNS are of two main types: COMMON NOUNS and PROPER NOUNS. PROPER NOUNS, such as personal names or the names of, say, cities, are words that are usually begun with a capital letter, for example:

'John', 'Mary', 'Dunedin', 'Wellington'.

Almost all nouns in an ordinary English dictionary are common nouns, but distinctions can sometimes be blurred. For instance, the word 'daisy' is a common noun when denoting the flower, but when used as a person's name — 'Daisy' — it becomes a proper noun.

A great number of English words used as verbs are also used as nouns: 'talk', 'book', 'dance' for example. But some words are used only as verbs (for example, 'speak', 'sing') and some are used only as nouns (for example, 'speech', 'song').

Many verbs in *te reo Māori* (such as *kōrero* and *waiata*, as noted above) may be used also as nouns. The words in the classes of nouns given below are words that are **not** used as verbs.

For instance, the Māori word *ika* ('fish') is not used as a verb in the way in which the English word 'fish' may be used, in the sense of 'to go fishing'. Quite different words, such as *hī* ('to fish with a line') or *hao* ('to fish with a net') are used for the verb.

In contrast to the two types of noun in English (common nouns and proper nouns) in *te reo Māori* NOUNS are of **three** main types.

COMMON NOUNS	PERSONAL NOUNS	LOCATION NOUNS
EXAMPLES	EXAMPLES	EXAMPLES
whare ('house')	*Mere*	*Otepōti*
ika ('fish')	*Hoani*	*Poneke*
rākau ('stick')	*Rewi*	*runga* ('top')
hīpi ('sheep')	*koe* ('you')	*mua* ('front')
kupu ('word')	*tātou* ('us all')	*uta* ('shore')

Thus, personal names and place names (both of which in English belong in the single class of 'proper nouns') are, in *te reo Māori*, divided between the two classes of PERSONAL NOUNS and LOCATION NOUNS.

The PERSONAL PRONOUNS (represented by *koe* and *tātou* in the list above) form a sub-class of PERSONAL NOUNS.

Also to be noted is that, in the class of LOCATION NOUNS, there is a small group of words (represented above by the words *runga*, *mua* and *uta*) that have no exact parallels in English.

The reason nouns in *te reo Māori* are classified in these three types is because they differ, one type from the other, in the way they are used in the construction of phrases and sentences. Separate chapters are given to each type, with more detailed explanations of the ways in which they are used, in Part III of this book.

THE PARTICLES

There are only a few PARTICLES (about 60 in total, the exact number depends on how many different functions of identical words are counted as separate words), and new words are not added to this list. It is the various **functions** of each that need to be understood.

When translating the meaning of a phrase or sentence from *te reo* into English **sometimes** an English word may be appropriate as a translation of a certain Māori PARTICLE, as has been shown to be the case with the phrase *ki te whare* ('to the house') where the PARTICLES *ki* and *te* are appropriately translated by 'to' and 'the' respectively. But it would be quite wrong to assume from this that, for instance, the Māori particle *ki* and the English word 'to' always correspond in function.

In some cases a different English word may be needed to translate *ki*, and in other cases *ki* may have a function in the Māori text for which there is no equivalent in English. It should again be emphasised, therefore, that, in relation to particles, rather than any translatable 'meaning', it is the various **structural** or **grammatical functions** of each, in different contexts that need to be understood. The most common of these functions — and many of the particles have multiple functions — are described in later chapters on the various groups of particles.

OTHER TYPES OF WORDS

Almost all of the words in the lexicon of *te reo Māori* may be classified as either BASE WORDS or PARTICLES. However, there are a number of very common words that evade such classification. Ray Harlow, in his *A Māori Reference Grammar* (pp. 39–41) provides information about such words, the list of which includes *āe* ('yes'), *kāo* ('no'), *engari* ('but') and *ahakoa* ('although').

Also to be mentioned here are words known as '*t*-class' DETERMINERS, which may be used **either** as particles (when preceding a noun) **or** as base words (when used as PRONOUNS), as well as those words known as '*t*-class' POSSESSIVE DETERMINERS (see chapter 13).

Words such as *tēnei* ('this') and *tētahi* ('one') are called '*t*-class' because the singular form of each begins with a '*t*', and this '*t*' is dropped to indicate a plural: *ēnei* ('these') and *ētahi* ('some').

In this book these words, in whatever situation they occur, are shown in bold print:

… *tēnei whare* …
this house

Ko te whare	*o Rewi*	*tēnei.*
the house	of Rewi	this

('This is Rewi's house.')

It could be noted that the English translations of such words, for example, 'this', 'one', 'some' — have a similar dual use: introducing nouns **or** acting as PRONOUNS.

A REVIEW OF WORD CLASSIFICATION

In dictionaries words are classified according to the manner in which they function as a 'part of speech' — that is, as NOUN, VERB, PREPOSITION and so on. It should be stressed that it is **usage** that determines classification, not vice-versa. But knowing how a given word is classified is helpful in that this supplies (in reverse as it were) the information as to how the word is normally used in a sentence.

On checking the pages of a dictionary (English or Māori) it is immediately apparent that most words have more than one classification. Only a small proportion of words are identified as belonging to a single class.

In English, words such as 'song' and 'food' are classed as NOUNS (they are 'naming words') while words such as 'sing' and 'eat' are classified as VERBS (they are 'doing words'). Other English words may be classified as ADJECTIVES, ADVERBS, PREPOSITIONS or other 'parts of speech'.

But the word 'talk', for instance, may function as a NOUN ('I went to hear the talk') **or** as a VERB ('Talk to me!') and a host of other English base words may, similarly, serve as more than one 'part of speech'.

A large number of English words are used as at least three or four different 'parts of speech'. The word 'hollow' for instance may serve as a NOUN, VERB, ADJECTIVE or even ADVERB (a word that 'qualifies' a verb), as in this sentence cited in the *New Zealand School Oxford Dictionary*: 'We beat them hollow.'

In English, words such as 'song' and 'food' are classed as NOUNS — and are used only as NOUNS; while words such as 'sing' and 'eat' are classed as VERBS — and are used only as VERBS. But a major proportion of English words have more than one function. Of particular frequency are words that are used as both NOUNS and VERBS.

When this system of classification is applied to *te reo Māori* something like the same situation is found — because many Māori base words may appear as the HEAD WORD of either a VERB PHRASE or a NOUN PHRASE, as with the word *kōrero* here:

Whakarongo	*ki te* **kōrero.**
Listen	to the speech (or talk).
Kōrero *mai*	*ki a* **au.**
Speak (or talk)	to me.

Functioning as a noun in the first sentence, and as a verb in the second, the Māori word *kōrero* is like the English 'talk', rather than like 'speech' (a NOUN only) or 'speak' (a VERB only).

The word *waiata* is seen to function as a verb ('singing') in a verb phrase or as a noun ('songs') in a noun phrase:

E **waiata** *ana*	*ngā* **tamariki**	*i ngā* **waiata.**
are singing	the children	the songs

('The children are singing the songs.')

It has already been emphasised that *te reo Māori* is strikingly different from English because it has two distinct main types of verb — called (in this book) ACTION VERBS and STATIVE VERBS. The word *pai* is used as a STATIVE VERB and is shown below functioning firstly as a verb (in a verb phrase) and secondly as a noun (in a noun phrase).

> *Ka pai*   *te mahi nei.*
> is good   the work here
>   ('This work is good.')
>
> *Ka nui*   *te pai!*
> is big   the good(ness)
>   ('Wonderful!' or 'Wow!')

But *pai*, like many other BASE WORDS, may also be **used** 'adjectivally' (that is, to describe something), as illustrated in the following sentence:

> *He whare pai*   *te whare nei.*
> a house good   the house here
>   ('This house is a good house.')

In this last example *pai* is not serving as the HEAD WORD in the phrase but simply 'qualifies' or describes the HEAD WORD *whare*, which is a COMMON NOUN (and thus the phrase '*He whare pai* ...' is classified as a NOUN PHRASE).

A FURTHER NOTE ABOUT ADJECTIVES AND VERBS

ADJECTIVES form an important class of words in English (and other languages). It is perhaps tempting to classify some Māori base words (such as *pai*) as adjectives — but it turns out to be quite difficult to determine exactly which words in *te reo* might belong in such a class.

In *te reo Māori* many words are used to 'qualify' nouns in the way adjectives do in English — although they usually follow rather than precede the NOUN, as in the phrase: *he whare pai* — 'a good house'.

Some authorities consider that words such as *pai* should be regarded as adjectives. This question of word classification is something important enough to review briefly here.

It is quite true that *pai*, and other words that are here called STATIVE VERBS, may be **used as** adjectives, for example:

He whare pai   *te whare nei.*

a house good   the house here

('This house is a good house.')

But words normally classified as COMMON NOUNS may also be used in the same manner, as is the common noun *kōhatu* in:

He whare kōhatu   *te whare nei.*

a house stone   the house here

('This house is a stone house.')

In fact, many words from three of the BASE WORD classes in *te reo* — ACTION VERBS, STATIVE VERBS and COMMON NOUNS — are **used** in this manner.

The 'adjectival nature' of words such as *pai* and *ora* has undoubtably been recognised by Bruce Biggs. In his *English–Maori,Maori–English Dictionary* these words are designated as 'stative-adjectives'.

In *The Oceanic Languages* by John Lynch, Malcolm Ross and Terry Crowley (Routledge, 2011, p. 63) it is asserted that in Proto-Oceanic (emphasis added here):

'There were **no adjectives as such**, just
adjectival verbs (a sub-class of **stative verb**) and a
small class of adjectival nouns (a sub-class of common noun).'

This view, which accords with that of Bruce Biggs, is now being increasingly recognised in writings on the grammar of *te reo*. Two sub-classes of stative verb are identified: an adjectival type (A-type) and a participle type (P-type).

There is no more reason for classifying Māori stative verbs as adjectives than there is for classifying English adjectives as stative verbs. As stressed at the beginning of this chapter, it is usage that determines the class of a word, and not vice-versa. The stative verbs of *te reo Māori* are used in very different ways to the limited ways in which English adjectives are used.

In English a descriptive phrase is usually made from an adjective (or participle) supported by a part of the verb 'to be'. No equivalent of the English verb 'to be' exists in *te reo Māori*, nor is one needed, because sentences of equivalent meaning can be made with stative verbs. That is how *te reo Māori* works, 'on its own terms'.

SUMMARY
Two classes of Verb
In *te reo Māori* two main classes of VERB are recognised. In this book they are called

ACTION VERBS and STATIVE VERBS

Many of these are **also used as** COMMON NOUNS.

THREE CLASSES OF NOUN

In English it is considered that there are **two** classes of NOUN: 'common nouns' and 'proper nouns'. In *te reo Māori* there are **three** classes of NOUN. None of these words are used as verbs.

COMMON NOUN   LOCATION NOUN   PERSONAL NOUN

(Since a PRONOUN is a word that 'stands in for' a noun, the class of PERSONAL NOUNS may be understood to include — as a sub-class — the PERSONAL PRONOUNS).

THE PARTICLES

Most, but not all, of the PARTICLES in *te reo* — about 60 in total — may be classified in one or other of **four** main groups: DETERMINERS, PREPOSITIONS, VERB PARTICLES and ADVERBIAL PARTICLES. More details follow in the specific chapters allotted to the PARTICLES.

Ultimately, of course, what is most important is not how a word is classified, but knowing how to use it correctly and effectively.

PART 3

The new grammar

SECTION A: BASE WORDS

5
Action verbs

ONE

ACTION VERBS denote **actions** — whether performed by people, animals or other things (rain, for instance, can **fall**; lightning can **strike**).

In English the form of a verb may change according to who or what is performing the action; and also according to the timeframe within which the action is performed.

The English verb 'go', for instance, changes (in the present TENSE) to 'goes' for the **3rd person singular** ('I **go**'; 'you **go**'; but 'he/she/it **goes**').

Changes to indicate the timeframe (or TENSE) are even more marked, with the forms '**gone**' and '**went**' for past TENSES, while for other TENSES (past, present or future) supplementary words are used in the verb phrase, for example, 'I am going'; 'he will go'; 'she might have gone.'

All VERBS in *te reo Māori* are **vastly simpler** than verbs in English (and many other languages). In *te reo* the form of the VERB itself (that is, the BASE WORD) **does not alter** either for PERSON or for TENSE. In the examples following it can be seen that while the form of the English verb changes from 'go' to 'going' to 'gone' and to 'went', the Māori verb *haere* remains unaltered.

*Ka **haere** au.*	('I go.' or 'I will go.')
*E **haere** ana ia.*	('He, or she, is, was or will be going.)
*Kua **haere** rātou.*	('They have gone.')
*I **haere** a **Tamahae**.*	('Tamahae went.')

In *te reo Māori* it is the verb particles associated with the base word in a verb phrase that change.

Although Māori verb phrases may be translated into specific tenses in English, it should not be assumed that the Māori verb particles create 'tenses' that exactly parallel the tenses of English verbs. *Te reo Māori* should not be forced into conformity with the patterns of English in such a manner.

This is an important point. It is very relevant to the comments made by Karena Kelly in her essay 'Iti te Kupu, Nui te Korero' (mentioned in the introduction) regarding the danger of *te reo* losing its distinctive features to become just a copy or, as she puts it 'a clone of English, a mere hybridised shadow' of the language it once was. The issue is addressed further in the section on verb particles in chapter 12.

TWO

Actions may be either TRANSITIVE or INTRANSITIVE. This means that the class of base words called action verbs is composed of two sub-classes:

TRANSITIVE VERBS and INTRANSITIVE VERBS

TRANSITIVE VERBS

When an action directly affects something or someone other than the 'doer' of the action, the verb is said to be TRANSITIVE. That is, the action passes from the 'doer' to something or someone else:

*Ka **patu***	*te **kōtiro***	*i te **paoro**.*
hits	the girl	the ball

('The girl hits the ball.')

*Ka **mōhio***	*ngā **tāngata***	*ki ngā **tikanga**.*
know	the people	the protocol

('The people know the protocol.')

The person who, or the thing which, **does** the action is called the SUBJECT in a sentence. The person who, or thing which, is affected by the action is called the OBJECT in the sentence.

The OBJECT of a TRANSITIVE VERB is known as a DIRECT OBJECT (that is, it's directly affected by the action).

Put another way: a TRANSITIVE VERB is an ACTION VERB that 'takes' — in fact requires — a DIRECT OBJECT.

It is noticeable that in each of the Māori sentences above the OBJECT PHRASE is connected to the sentence by the type of word called a PREPOSITION (*i* in the first instance, and *ki* in the second) while in the English translations no prepositions are used.

INTRANSITIVE VERBS

When an action does not directly affect anything or anyone other than the 'doer' the verb is said to be INTRANSITIVE:

*E **haere** ana*	*te **rangatira**.*
is going	the chief

('The chief is going.')

Kei te **moe**   te **tamaiti**.
is sleeping   the child
('The child is sleeping.')

DIRECT AND INDIRECT OBJECTS

INTRANSITIVE VERBS do not take DIRECT OBJECTS. They may, however, take INDIRECT OBJECTS:

E **haere** ana   te **kōtiro**   ki te **tāone**.
is going   the girl   to the town
('The girl is going to town.')

In fact, both TRANSITIVE and INTRANSITIVE VERBS may take INDIRECT OBJECTS:

Ka **patu**   te **tamaiti**   i te **paoro**   ki te **taiapa**.
hits   the child   the ball   to the fence
('The child hits the ball to the fence.')

What is to be noticed is that in both English and *te reo* an INDIRECT OBJECT is preceded by a PREPOSITION. In English no PREPOSITION precedes a DIRECT OBJECT, but in *te reo Māori* one is required.

In *te reo Māori* all OBJECT PHRASES are connected to sentences by PREPOSITIONS. The PREPOSITION used most often is *i*, but in some cases it is *ki*. (Further information will be found in chapter 12 in the section on the PREPOSITIONS.)

THREE
PASSIVE VERBS

Both TRANSITIVE and INTRANSITIVE VERBS may be used in either the **active** or the **passive** 'voice'. This applies both to *te reo Māori* and to English.

When the SUBJECT (whoever or whatever) of a sentence is 'doing' the action, a VERB is being used **actively**. (The SUBJECT is the 'actor'.) When, on the other hand, the action is being 'done to', whoever or whatever is the SUBJECT of the sentence the VERB is being used **passively**. The SUBJECT, in this situation, is the 'passive' recipient of the action.

The first sentence below shows the word *kōrero* being used **actively**: *te wahine* is the SUBJECT, and she is **doing** the action of speaking.

E *kōrero ana*	*te wahine*	*i te karakia*.
is speaking	the woman	the prayer

('The woman is speaking the prayer.')

The next sentence shows the same word (with a passive suffix added) being used **passively**: *te karakia* has now become the SUBJECT, and it is **being spoken by** the woman, who is now called the AGENT.

E *kōrerotia ana*	*te karakia*	*e te wahine*.
is spoken	the prayer	by the woman

('The prayer is spoken by the woman.')

The difference in meaning between the sentences is simply a difference in emphasis. In an active sentence the emphasis is more on **who** (or what) is **doing** the action. In a passive sentence the emphasis is more on **to whom** (or what) the action is **done**.

In a passive sentence it is the SUBJECT rather than an OBJECT that is affected by the action.

This is the case with INTRANSITIVE VERBS as much as with TRANSITIVE VERBS. In a sense INTRANSITIVE VERBS become TRANSITIVE when used in the passive voice. That is, the SUBJECT is something, or someone, affected by the action.

The INTRANSITIVE VERB *haere* ('to go' or 'to travel') has the passive form *haerea*, with a meaning something like 'be travelled over' (see Williams' dictionary, p. xxxvi) as in:

Kua **haerea**   te **ara** ra.
has been travelled   the pathway yonder.
('That pathway has been travelled.')

One of the differences between *te reo* and English is highlighted here. In *te reo* the VERB PHRASE comes first in both active and passive sentences. This suggests that **what** is **being done** is considered to be of primary importance in both cases.

(But a notable instance in *te reo* of a shift in emphasis from 'action' to 'actor', is found in the 'actor emphatic' construction. See chapter 16.)

In *te reo* the sequence of the phrases that follow the verb phrase may, however, often be varied. In the sentence quoted earlier from *The Book of Revelation* the passive construction is also found, but here the SUBJECT PHRASE — *he awa wai ora* — is in the fourth position in the sequence of phrases, while the AGENT PHRASE — e *ia* — occupies the second position:

Ka whakakitea mai	*e ia*	*ki ahau*
shown	by him	to me
he awa wai ora	*pīata tonu*	*me te karāihe*
a river water life	clear very	as the crystal.
e puta mai ana	*i te torōna*	*o te Atua.*
emerging	from the throne	of the God.

It has been noted by several writers that there is a stronger tendency towards using the passive form in *te reo* than there is in English. Indicative of this, perhaps, is the fact that the English version of the same sentence is expressed in the active form: 'He showed me a river of the water of life ...'

THE FORM OF THE PASSIVE SUFFIX

It has been mentioned that when ACTION VERBS are used in the PASSIVE VOICE a passive suffix (or ending) is usually added to the verb.

Passive suffixes always end in -*a*, but they may, according to Williams' dictionary, take any of the following forms:

-a, -hanga, -hia, -hina, -ina, -kia, -kina, -mia, -na, -nga, -ngia, -ria, -rina, -tia, -whia, -whina and (rarely) -*ea*.

Because there seems to be no comprehensive rules for determining which passive suffix is normally attached to any particular verb, it is useful to try to memorise the correct form of the passive with each new ACTION VERB encountered.

Both transitive and intransitive verbs are commonly shown in dictionaries each accompanied by its usual passive suffix in the following manner:

aroha (-*ina*)	'to love'	
kai (-*nga*)	'to eat'	
kōrero (-*tia*)	'to speak'	

Thus, *arohaina* means 'to be loved':

I arohaina	*a Hinemoa*	*e Tūtanekai*.
was loved	Hinemoa	by Tūtanekai.

('Hinemoa was loved by Tūtanekai.')

Kainga means 'to be eaten':

*Kua **kainga***	*te **parāoa***	*e ngā **rakiraki**.*
has been eaten	the bread	by the ducks

('The bread has been eaten by the ducks.')

Kōrerotia means 'to be spoken':

*E **kōrerotia** ana*	*te **karakia***	*e te **wahine**.*
is spoken	the prayer	by the woman

('The prayer is spoken by the woman.')

FURTHER COMMENTS ON THE PASSIVE

There are several further details concerning variations in passive constructions that are beyond the scope of this elementary book. Both Ray Harlow's *A Māori Reference Grammar* and Winifred Bauer's *The Reed Reference Grammar of Māori* provide more extensive information. But a few comments, at least, should be added here.

- Where the first syllable or syllables of a verb are reduplicated, the duplication is normally dropped from the passive form (and the whole form of the passive is normally shown in dictionaries) thus:

pupuhi (***pūhia***)	'to blow'
titiro (***tirohia***)	'to see'
tuhituhi (***tuhia***)	'to write'

- The passive form may be used as an **imperative** — that is, to give a command or instruction:

  Nohoia! ('Sit down!')

(More about imperatives is to be found in chapter 7.)

- A few VERBS, such as *hōmai* do not take passive endings even when being used in a passive sense.

Other variations of passive sentences need to be considered individually. Ray Harlow makes a special case for constructions using *taea* (which may perhaps rather clumsily be translated as 'to be enabled').

The use of *taea* is illustrated by the well-known proverb:

He tao rākau,	*ka taea te karo;*
a spear wooden,	enabled (is) the parrying

he tao kī,	*e kore e taea te karo.*
a spear spoken	cannot be enabled the parrying

('A wooden spear can be parried;
a spoken word spear cannot be parried.')

A further type of passive construction (called 'pseudo-passive' in Ray Harlow's grammar) is formed by using the phrase *He mea* followed by a verb (without any passive ending). A notable example of this construction is found as the opening sentence of the current version of *Te Paipera Tapu* ('Holy Bible'):

He mea hanga	*nā te Atua*	*i te tīmatanga*
created	by the God	was in the beginning

te rangi	*me te whenua,*
the heaven	and the earth.

('In the beginning God created the heaven and the earth.')

6
Stative verbs

Words such as *tūpato* ('to be careful'), *ora* ('to be alive and well'), *pai* ('to be good or fine'), *mutu* ('to be finished', in the sense of 'ceased'), *mahue* ('to be left behind') and *rangatira* ('to be esteemed') are considered to be STATIVE VERBS. They express, or refer to, the **state** of someone or something. (In some books these VERBS are just called STATIVES.)

STATIVE VERBS are used with the same particles as ACTION VERBS.

Here are some examples of simple sentences with STATIVE VERBS used with various VERB PARTICLES.

*Ka **pai** tēnā!*
good that
('That's good!')

*Kia **ora** e **koe**!*
be alive and well you
('May you be well!')

*Kua **mutu** te **kura**.*
has finished the school
('School has finished.')

STATIVE VERBS are also (as are ACTION VERBS) commonly used in constructions beginning with either of the PREPOSITIONS *kei* or *i* followed by the DEFINITE ARTICLE *te* (*kei* for present tense and *i* for past):

*Kei te **pai***   *ahau.*

good   I

('I'm fine.')

STATIVE VERBS are of two main types: adjective-type (or A-type) and participle-type (or P-type).

VERB PHRASES in *te reo* that use A-type stative verbs are commonly translated into English by verb phrases comprised of some part of the verb 'to be' followed by an adjective.

*Kei te **pai*** …	('… am/is/are good.')
*Kua **tūreiti*** …	('… am/is/are late.')
*Ka **roa*** …	('… am/is/are/will be long.')

Participles, in English, are words derived from verbs and used in 'compound' tenses. From the verb 'to finish', for instance, are derived the present participle 'finishing' (used in compound tenses such as 'is finishing' and 'was finishing') and the past participle 'finished' (used in such compound tenses as 'is finished' and 'was finished').

VERB PHRASES in *te reo* that use P-type stative verbs are commonly translated into English by verb phrases comprised of some part of the verb 'to be' and/or some part of the verb 'to have' followed by a participle.

*Kei te **ngaro*** …	('… is/are missing.')
*Kua **mutu*** …	('… have/has finished.')
*Kua **mahue*** …	('… have/has been left behind.')

But Māori A-type stative verbs are distinguished from the P-type not by the class of word used in translation, but by the differences in the ways they are used in *te reo*.

A-type stative verbs (for example, *whero, pai, ora, rangatira*) are often used simply to 'qualify' a noun — as are adjectives in English — but in *te reo* they are usually placed after the noun.

> *he whare whero* ('a red house')
> *te reo rangatira* ('the esteemed language')

Māori stative verbs of the P-type differ from the A-type in that they do not seem to be used simply to 'qualify' nouns, but are used only in separate phrases.

> Kua ***mutu***   *te **kura***.
> has finished   the school
> ('School has finished.')

> Kua ***mahue***   *te **kurī***.
> has been left behind   the dog
> ('The dog's been left behind.')

When stative verbs are used with the indefinite article *he* a translation often has a VERBAL sense.

> He *whero*   *te **whare***.
> is red   the house
> ('The house is red.')

This would seem to indicate that while the particle *he* is usually regarded as a DETERMINER (the 'indefinite article') perhaps it should be understood as serving sometimes as VERB PARTICLE (see chapter 12).

In other situations, however, translation by a NOUN may be more appropriate. For instance, while the sentence *He **rangatira** a **Rewi**.* might, perhaps, be translated as 'Rewi is esteemed.' it is probably much more likely to be rendered: 'Rewi is a chief.'

Many STATIVE VERBS are, in fact, often used as COMMON NOUNS:

*te **pai*** ('the goodness'); *te **ora*** ('the life and health'); *te **roa*** ('the length'); *te **rangatira*** ('the chief').

But in many cases 'noun-endings' are added to the basic verb, for example:

*te **oranga*** ('the well-being'); *te **mutunga*** ('the finish').

The **derivation** of COMMON NOUNS — from both ACTION VERBS and STATIVE VERBS — in this manner is explored more fully in the next chapter.

Also in the next chapter is some description of the function of two prefixes: *whaka-* and *kai-*, which are frequently attached to verbs. Of particular interest is that attaching the prefix *whaka-* to a STATIVE VERB **changes it** into an ACTION VERB. (See next chapter.)

NUMERALS

The numerals in *te reo Māori* are a sub-class of STATIVE VERBS, and are used with VERB PARTICLES.

In *A Māori Reference Grammar*, Ray Harlow assigns a chapter (chapter 8) to 'Numerals and time expressions' because, he says, they 'have such complex forms of expression in Māori, and … differ … so much from English equivalents'. For anything like a comprehensive coverage of the topic Ray Harlow's book is invaluable.

Here, only a few of the main points about the use of numerals are noted.

The cardinal numbers 1 to 10 are:

tahi, rua, toru, whā, rima, ono, whitu, waru, iwa, tekau

The word *kore* is used for 0 (zero)
To refer to numbers over 10 the particle *mā* ('plus') is used:

tekau mā tahi (11)
tekau mā rua (12) and so on,

and the numbers are compounded in this fashion up to 100:

rua tekau mā tahi (21),
ono tekau mā waru (68) and so on until
kotahi rau (100).

When stating 'how many' of anything *tahi* is prefixed by *ko-*, and the numbers 2–9 (**not** *tekau*) are preceded by the verb particle *e*:

Kotahi anake   te *pukapuka*.
One only   the book
('There is only one book.')

E rua   ngā *pukapuka*.
two   the books
('There are two books.')

Tekau mā   *rima*   ngā *whare*.
('There are fifteen houses.')

In stating 'how many people' (numbers 2–9 only) the 'human prefix' *toko* is used:

Tokorima ngā *tamariki*.

In counting **things** one-by-one the verb particle *ka* may be used:

*Ka **tahi**,*	*ka **rua**,*	*ka **toru**,*	*ka **whā*** and so on.
one	two	three	four and so on.

The ordinal numbers from 1st to 9th are formed by prefixing *tua-* to the cardinals 1–9:

te **tuatahi** ('the first'), *te* **tuarua** ('the second') and so on.

The question for asking 'How many?' is *E **hia*** (for things):

*E **hia***	*ngā **rākau whero**?*
How many	the sticks red?

('How many red sticks are there?')

but for people ***hia*** is prefixed with *toko-*:

Tokohia	*ngā **tangata**?*
How many	the people?

(See also chapter 16.)

7
Some further verb constructions

THE 'CAUSATIVE' PREFIX *WHAKA-*

Both action verbs and stative verbs may be modified with the so-called 'causative' prefix *whaka-*. 'Causative', as the word suggests, carries the sense of **causing** something to happen or take place.

So, one of the meanings of the action verb *rongo* is 'to hear'; and the meaning of *whakarongo* is 'to cause to hear or to be heard (by the act of listening)' or, simply, 'to listen'.

The action verb *haere* means 'to move' (usually 'to go' except when followed by the directional particle *mai*, which signifies 'hither' — and the phase *Haere mai!* thus means 'Move hither!' or ' Come this way!'); and the word *whakahaere* means 'to cause to go' / 'to organise'.

The stative verb *pai* means 'to be good or fine'. *Whakapai* means 'to make (something) good', 'to make tidy' or even 'to bless (something)'.

Stative verbs do not, normally, take passive endings (their meaning, as Bruce Biggs has pointed out, is always, in a sense, passive). But, as can be seen in the above example of *pai*, when a stative verb is prefixed by *whaka-* it is **converted into** an ACTION VERB.

Passive endings (as shown in brackets in the examples below) may then be added:

whakatūpato (-ria)	'to warn' (cause to be careful)
whakaroa (-tia)	'to lengthen' (cause to be long)
whakaora (-ngia/-tia)	'to cure' (cause to be healthy)
whakamutu (-a)	'to stop' (cause to be finished)

As with any action verbs, the passive forms can be used to give instructions or commands.

Whakapaitia (or *-ngia*)   *te ruma!*
('Cause to be good' (or 'tidy') 'the room!')

Whakamutua!
('Cause something to finish' or 'Stop that!')

E te Atua,	*whakapaingia*	*ēnei kai* ...
O Lord	bless	these foods ...

Instructions may also be given by using the simple form of a verb:

Haere! ('Go!')

or a verb prefixed by *whaka-*:

Whakarongo! ('Listen!')

with or without a following DIRECTIONAL PARTICLE:

Haere mai!	('Come here!')
Haere atu!	('Go away!')

Whakarongo mai! ('Listen here!')

Karanga mai! ('Call in this direction!')

Where the verb has no more than two short vowels, or one long one, and is being used to give an instruction, command or direction, it is usually preceded by the particle *e*. So:

Haere! ('Go!')

Whakarongo! ('Listen!')

but

*E **tū**.* ('Stand up.')

*E **noho**.* ('Sit down' or 'Take a seat.')

This *e* may be omitted if the verb is to be **followed** by another particle, thus:

Noho mai. ('Sit here.')

COMMON NOUNS DERIVED FROM VERBS

A large proportion of base words in *te reo*, both action verbs and stative verbs, are used also as COMMON NOUNS, for example:

waiata ('song'); *kōrero* ('speech'); *mahi* ('job');
ora ('life'/'health'); *pai* ('goodness').

Such words, like the English words 'talk', 'walk', 'run', 'dance' and many others, thus function as more than just one 'part of speech'.

In many cases, however, what are called 'noun-endings' are added to base words. Noun-endings' always terminate in *-nga*, but may take any of the following forms:

-nga -anga -hanga -inga -kanga -manga -ranga -tanga
-whanga

When a 'noun-ending' is attached, a base word becomes a common noun, and is used **only** as a common noun.

So, although the stative verb *ora* ('to be alive and healthy') may, itself, serve as a common noun ('life'/'health') when a noun-ending (in this case *-nga*) is attached a further noun *oranga* ('well-being' or 'sustenance') is formed.

E te Atua,	*whakapaingia*	*ēnei kai,*
O Lord	bless	these foods
hei oranga	*mō ō mātou*	*tinana* …
as sustenance	for our	bodies …

Similarly:

tangi ('to cry')   *te tangi* ('the cry')
           te tangihanga ('the occasion of crying'/'the funeral')

rangatira ('to be   *te rangatira* ('the chief')
esteemed')   *te rangatiratanga* ('the chieftainship or sovereignty')

8
Common nouns

Base words that are classified exclusively as COMMON NOUNS are those base words that may be **directly preceded** by the DEFINITE ARTICLE — *te* — but which are **not used as verbs**.

Common nouns in *te reo* are base words that give **names** to objects and things in the world of experience, including even such 'things' as mental concepts.

Excluded from this class, however, are those names that are classified either as PERSONAL NOUNS or as LOCATION NOUNS (see the next two chapters respectively).

Words such as *ika* ('fish'), *kōhatu* or *kōwhatu* ('stone'), *kōtiro* ('girl'), *manu* ('bird'), *rākau* ('tree', 'stick') and *whare* ('house', 'building') are examples of common nouns, and are used **only** as common nouns. Therefore, *te rākau* ('the tree' or 'stick'); *te ika* ('the fish'); *te manu* ('the bird'); *te kōwhatu* ('the stone').

In *te reo Māori*, as in English, there are many words that are **used** as **either** VERBS **or** COMMON NOUNS. This means that the words which are actually classified as COMMON NOUNS (that is, **not** used as VERBS) are, therefore, only a small proportion of the total number of words that may be **used as** COMMON NOUNS.

But it is still useful to know when a word is actually **classified** as a COMMON NOUN (rather than just knowing that it may be **used**

as a COMMON NOUN) because this supplies the information that the word is restricted in its use.

The classification of (for instance) the word *ika* ('fish') as a COMMON NOUN, makes it clear that *ika* is not used in the same manner as the English word 'fish' (which serves as both noun and verb). In *te reo*, reference to the action of 'fishing' employs quite different words, which are ACTION VERBS — such as *hī* ('to fish with a line') or *hao* ('to fish with a net').

Virtually all the information given here about common nouns in *te reo* applies also to the words from either of the two verb classes, when they are being **used as** common nouns, with or without the addition of a 'noun-ending' (see previous chapter).

✕✕✕

Almost all common nouns have the same form for singular and plural. (In this respect, they are similar to the English words 'sheep' and 'deer'.) For example:

ngā **manu** ('the birds'); *ngā* **ika** ('the fish');

ngā **kōtiro** ('the girls'); *ngā* **whare** ('the houses');

ngā **waiata** ('the songs'); *ngā* **rangatira** ('the chiefs').

The very few comon nouns that do show a change are all words referring to people, and, for all of them except *tamaiti* ('child') the change involves simply the lengthening of a vowel-sound for the plural.

Singular		Plural
matua	('parent')	*mātua*
taina or *teina*	('younger sister of a female or younger brother of a male')	*tāina* or *tēina*
tuakana	('older sister of a female or older brother of a male')	*tuākana*
tuahine	('sister of a male')	*tuāhine*
tipuna or *tupuna*	('ancestor')	*tīpuna* or *tūpuna*
wahine	('woman')	*wāhine*
tangata	('person')	*tāngata*
tamaiti	('child')	*tamariki*

Any PHRASE in which a COMMON NOUN occurs as the HEAD WORD is a NOUN PHRASE. Examples of NOUN PHRASES and SENTENCES in which NOUN PHRASES occur will be found throughout this book.

✕✕✕

In English grammar it is sometimes stressed that the essential requirement for a sentence to be considered complete is that there is a main verb. This rule does not apply in relation to *te reo Māori*.

Complete sentences in *te reo* often consist simply of two NOUN PHRASES, for example:

*He **mahi pai*** te **mahi** nei.

work good   the work here

('This work is good work.')

*Ko **Hongi*** te **rangatira**.

Hongi   the chief.

('Hongi is the chief.')

The *te reo* sentences are entirely clear and complete in meaning, but it should be noted that fluent English translations of these sentences are made by introducing the linking verb 'is'. There is no equivalent of this linking verb, nor is it needed, in *te reo Māori*.

Similarly, there is no equivalent in English of the Māori PREPOSITION *ko* (in the phrase *Ko **Hongi*** above). *Ko* certainly does not mean 'is'. This word has been called 'a specifying particle' (in *Te **Rangatahi***). In *LLM* (and in this book) it is called the FOCUS PREPOSITION.

But another point to note in relation to the above two sentences is the apparent difference in the PHRASE-SEQUENCE between the first example and the second.

In the first sentence the SUBJECT PHRASE (*te **mahi** nei* — 'this work') is in the usual second position; but in the second sentence the order of the phrases has been reversed, and the SUBJECT PHRASE (*Ko **Hongi*** — 'Hongi') occupies the first position.

It is probably possible to translate the second sentence as 'The chief is Hongi' — in which case it might seem that *te **rangatira*** ('the chief') is the subject — but the preference here is to regard the construction as an example of what in Ray Harlow's *Reference Grammar* is called a 'fronted subject', where the subject is brought into 'focus'.

Ko acts as a 'pointer' or 'marker', to focus attention on the NOUN that follows. Further information on the uses of *ko* is in chapter 12 in the section on PREPOSITIONS.

Most — perhaps all — COMMON NOUNS may be placed after the HEAD WORD in a phrase to 'qualify' that word. For example:

he awa wai ora ('a river of life-giving water')
and
te whare kōwhatu ('the stone house').

A great number of the COMMON NOUNS in the lexicon of *te reo Māori* today are words adopted from other languages — mostly English — particularly the names of things that were unknown to the Māori prior to the arrival of Europeans. These words are called 'transliterations' and are identified as such in *He Pātaka Kupu* by the words *reo kē* ('other language'). Transliterations are considered more fully in chapter 1 on the sounds and the written form of *te reo*.

9
Personal nouns and personal pronouns

The personal names of people (for example, *Rangi, Kiri, Pita,* Thomas) are PERSONAL NOUNS. Houses, canoes, weapons and other things, including the months of the year are also given individual names which are PERSONAL NOUNS (for example, *Mataatua,* which is the name of one of the ancestral canoes or *waka,* and also the name of a meeting house).

PERSONAL NOUNS in *te reo* are usually directly preceded by either the PERSONAL ARTICLE *a,* as in:

<blockquote>

Ka haere   *a Mere.*   ('Mary goes.')

</blockquote>

or a PREPOSITION:

<blockquote>

Ko Rewi   *te rangatira.*   ('Rewi is the chief.')
Mā Mere   *tēnei ika.*   ('This fish is for Mary.')

</blockquote>

Following any of the LOCATION PREPOSITIONS, *ki, kei, i* or *hei,* PERSONAL NOUNS **and** PERSONAL PRONOUNS are directly preceded by the PERSONAL ARTICLE *a.* There is no counterpart to this word in English.

Hōatu	*te rākau*	*ki a **Mere**.*
Give	the stick	to Mary.

Hōmai	*te rākau*	*ki a au.*
Give	the stick	to me.

An exception to this rule is that the *a* is omitted when variant forms — such as *ahau* or *awau* — of the first person singular PERSONAL PRONOUN are used.

Hōmai	*te rākau*	*ki ahau.*
Give	the stick	to me.

PERSONAL NOUNS, **but not** PERSONAL PRONOUNS, are directly preceded by this *a* when they are the unemphasised SUBJECT of a sentence.

Ka haere	*a **Mere**.*	('Mary goes.')
but		
Ka haere	*au.*	('I go.')

When they are not preceded by the PERSONAL ARTICLE, PERSONAL NOUNS are usually preceded by a PREPOSITION.

*Ko **Rewi***	*te hoa*	*o **Mere**.*
Rewi	the friend	of Mary.

('Rewi is Mary's friend.')

In cases where the DEFINITE ARTICLE, *te*, forms part of a personal name, this article is treated simply as part of the name in any construction.

<blockquote>

Ka haere a Te Rauparaha. ('Te Rauparaha goes.')

Ko Te Kooti te rangatira. ('Te Kooti is the chief.')

</blockquote>

THE PERSONAL PRONOUNS

The PERSONAL PRONOUNS form a sub-group of the PERSONAL NOUNS. They are a small set of words that are used so frequently that a thorough familiarity with them must be considered essential at even the most elementary level of *te reo Māori*.

There are 11 words (not counting variant forms, such as *ahau*) in the set of PERSONAL PRONOUNS in *te reo*, and two associated words — *wai* and *mea* — which are discussed separately.

To a speaker of English, the Māori system of PERSONAL PRONOUNS, because it is so different from English, may initially seem confusing — even though there are just the same number of words (11) in each system.

Charts of the schemes of the personal pronouns, of both English and *te reo Māori* respectively, are given here for purposes of comparison.

ENGLISH Personal Pronouns				
	Singular		**Plural**	
	SUBJECT	OBJECT	SUBJECT	OBJECT
1st person	I	me	we	us
2nd person	you	you	you	you
3rd person	he/she	him/her	they	them

PERSONAL PRONOUNS of *TE REO MĀORI*		
	SUBJECT OR OBJECT		
	1 PERSON	2 PEOPLE	3 OR MORE
1st person 'inclusive'		*tāua* 'we'/'us'	*tātou* 'we'/'us'
1st person 'exclusive'	*au* or *ahau* 'I'/'me'	*māua* 'we'/'us'	*mātou* 'we'/'us'
2nd person	*koe* 'you'	*kōrua* 'you'	*koutou* 'you'
3rd person	*ia* 'he'/'she' 'him'/'her'	*rāua* 'they'/'them'	*rātou* 'they'/'them'

The Māori PERSONAL PRONOUNS shown in the above chart are standard forms, but it should be noted that several variant forms are also in use such as *awau* (instead of *au* or *ahau*) and *tātau* (instead of *tātou*).

The following comments may be checked by referring back to the charts.

PERSONAL PRONOUNS in English distinguish:
- (a) SUBJECT from OBJECT (in all cases except the 2nd person)
- (b) GENDER (in the 3rd person singular)
- (c) **Two** NUMBERS (singular and plural)
- (d) **Three** PERSONS (1st, 2nd and 3rd).

PERSONAL PRONOUNS in *te reo Māori* do **not** distinguish either
- (a) SUBJECT from OBJECT or
- (b) GENDER.

They also radically differ from English in that they distinguish:
- (c) **Three** NUMBERS (1 person, 2 people and 3 or more people)
- (d) **Four** PERSONS (1st inclusive, 1st exclusive, 2nd and 3rd).

The inclusive forms **include the person or persons addressed** (that is, the person or people to whom 2nd person PERSONAL PRONOUNS refer); the exclusive forms do not include the person or people being addressed. Therefore:

au + *koe* = *tāua* (inclusive)
au + *kōrua* or *koutou* = *tātou* (inclusive)

but

au + *ia* = *māua* (exclusive)
au + *rāua* or *rātou* = *mātou* (exclusive)

The uses of *tāua* and *tātou* are straightforward: *tāua* means 'the two of us' (the person one is addressing and oneself); *tātou* means 'all of us' (the people one is addressing and oneself).

But when speaking or writing about a third person and oneself — when one wishes to say, for example, 'Mary and I ...', the correct construction is **not** '*Mere* (and) *au* ...' but:

māua   ko **Mere** ...

The literal sense of this construction is 'two of us, the person in addition to myself being Mary ...'

When wishing to say 'Mary, Tamahae and I ...' the construction is:

mātou   ko **Mere**   ko **Tamahae** ...

Translated literally, this is: 'us, the people in addition to myself being Mary and Tamahae ...'

Similarly, also:

kōrua	*ko **Mere***	('you two, the person in addition to you being
	...	Mary ...')
koutou	*ko **Mere*** *ko **Tamahae*** ...	('you, Mary and Tamahae ...')
Mere	*rāua*	*ko **Hata** ...* ('Mary and Hata ...')
Mere	*rātou*	*ko **Hata*** *ko **Tamahae** ...*
		('Mary, Hata and Tamahae ...')

In these kinds of construction it is not necessarily the personal **names** of people that are used. Here are some further examples:

māua	*ko **tōku hoa***	('my friend and I')
kōrua	*ko **tāu tane***	('you and your husband')
Mere	*rāua*	*ko **tōna hoa*** ('Mary and her friend')
mātou	*ko **ōku hoa***	('my friends and I')
koutou	*ko **tōu whanau***	('you and your family')
Hata	*rātou*	*ko **tōna whanau*** ('Hata and his family')

The use of personal pronouns in this way is so basic to *te reo Māori* (and so different to the way they are used in English) that it is well worth putting time into practicing these constructions. The first book of Hoani Waititi's *Te Rangatahi* series offers an excellent range of illustrations and practical exercises.

THE WORDS *WAI?* AND *MEA*

There are two other PERSONAL PRONOUNS to be considered.

wai?

This 'interrogative' personal pronoun is used to ask questions about a person or persons. Here are three examples of its use.

Ko wai	*tōu hoa?*	('Who is your friend?')

I kōrero	*a Hata*	*ki a wai?*
spoke	Hata	to whom

('To whom did Hata speak?')

Ko wai	*tōu ingoa?*	('What is your name?')

These examples provide a good illustration of the fact that while a particular English word may serve to translate a particular Māori word in one context, it may not necessarily be appropriate in another context.

The Māori word *wai?* does not actually **mean** 'who?' or 'whom?' It is a PERSONAL PRONOUN that is used in *te reo Māori* to ask about the identity of a person or persons. In English we do not say 'Who is your name?' But it is *te reo Māori* which is more consistent here. (This topic is taken up again under 'Asking questions' in chapter 18.)

mea

The word *mea* has at least six different uses. It serves as an ACTION VERB, with the meaning of 'to speak'. It serves as a COMMON NOUN, with the meaning of 'thing'. It is also used as a PERSONAL PRONOUN (with a meaning similar to the English 'so-and-so') when the name of a person about whom one talking is unknown, forgotten, or considered unimportant.

I mea atu	*ahau*	*ki a mea.*
spoke	I	to so-and-so

('I spoke to so-and-so.')

10
Location nouns

In *te reo Māori* all 'place' names (names of countries, cities, towns and so on) are classified as LOCATION NOUNS.

Also classified as LOCATION NOUNS are certain words (a group of some 30 or so) that refer to specific places or locations in space or time. These particular words, like place names, are not normally preceded directly by *he* ('a' or 'some') or by *te* ('the') or any other DETERMINER (see chapter 12). Note that there are exceptions, such as where *Te* is an integral part of the place name, for example, in *Te Kūiti* — and, for instance, in the phrase *te **Runga** Rawa* ('the above all', 'the highest power', that is, 'God').

LOCATION NOUNS are the **only** type of base word that may follow any of the LOCATION PREPOSITIONS (*ki, kei, i, hei*) directly.

As in English, one would not say 'at the Oamaru' but 'at Oamaru', so in *te reo Māori* the construction is not *kei te Ōamaru* but:

kei Ōamaru ('at Oamaru')

Words of the particular group mentioned above, such as ***runga*** ('the topside'), are used in the same manner:

*kei **runga** …*
at the topside

*kei **runga***   *i te **tēpu***
at the topside   of the table
('on the table')

The list that follows below comprises most of the commonly encountered examples of this type of word.

Each of the words is provided with an English 'gloss' (one or two words suggestive of the meaning), but many of these words have a considerable range of meanings.

Although **some** of them may be used in a 'stand alone' position in casual speech (for example, *āpōpō* — 'tomorrow') most of them will **always** be preceded by (or prefixed with) a PREPOSITION that completes a PHRASE. Often, such a phrase will have an idiomatic meaning well beyond what might be indicated by the bare 'glosses' given below (for example, *i reira* — 'there', 'then' and so on; *nō reira* — 'hence' and so on.)

runga	'the topside' (also 'the south')
raro	'the underside' (also 'the north')
mua	'the front side'
muri	'the back side' or 'the rear'
roto	'the inside'
waho	'the outside'
tāwāhi	'the other side' (of sea, river or valley)
tua	'the other side' (of, for example, a hill)
tai	'the sea', 'the shore from landward'
uta	'the inland', 'the shore from seaward'

waenga or *waenganui*	'the middle'
hea? or *whea?*	'where?'
kō	'yonder place'
konei	'here'
konā	'there' (near a person addressed)
korā	'there' (yonder)
reira	(place or time previously mentioned)
āianei	'now', 'today'
āpōpō	'tomorrow'
nanahi	'yesterday'
aoake	'the day before' or 'the day after'
neherā	'the ancient times'

Several other LOCATION NOUNS may be found (classified l.n. for 'local noun') in Williams' *Dictionary*.

In English there are prepositions such as 'on', 'in', 'under' and 'outside' for referring to the location of things — in such phrases as 'on the table' or 'outside the door'. Each of these statements is made with a **single phrase in English**, but in *te reo Māori*, by contrast, **two phrases** are required to supply the same information.

kei **runga**   *i te* **tēpu**
at topside   of the table
('on the table')

kei *waho*   *i te* **kuaha**
at outside   of the door
('outside the door')

85

Here are some further examples of LOCATION NOUN phrases and sentences.

*ki **runga***	*ki te **whenua***	('upon earth')
*Kei **whea***	***tāku pukapuka**?*	('Where's my book?')
*Kei **roto***	*i te **kāpata**.*	('In the cupboard.')
*Kei **konei**.*	('Here.'/'It's here.')	

*I **haere***	*ia*	*ki **runga***	*ki te **maunga**.*
went	he	upon	the mountain

('He went upon the mountain.')

SOME FURTHER POINTS

Because they are NOUNS, in many cases LOCATION NOUNS appear as the SUBJECT in sentences, where they are preceded by the same *a* that precedes PERSONAL NOUNS — as in, for instance this comment on the weather:

*Kei te **ātaahua***	*a **waho**.*
(It) is beautiful	outside

Such a sentence will follow the usual pattern of VERB PHRASE followed by SUBJECT PHRASE.

COMMON IDIOMS

*mā **runga***	***hoiho***	('on horseback')
*mā **runga***	***motokā***	('by motorcar')
*mā **raro***		('on foot')

✕✕✕

In some earlier books constructions such as:

*kei **roto** i ...* and *kei **runga** i ...*

are defined as 'complex prepositions'. This seems rather confusing. The English words 'in' and 'on' are prepositions, but the Māori constructions certainly are not. Literal, word-for-word, translation of the above two constructions would be as follows:

*kei **roto***	*i ...*	*kei **runga***	*i ...*
at inside	of	at topside	of

These constructions may correspond in **meaning**, respectively, to the English PREPOSITIONS 'in' and 'on', but in each case **three** Māori words are used.

The two words *kei **roto*** form a **complete** LOCATION PHRASE (that is, a LOCATION PREPOSITION followed by a LOCATION NOUN). The same may be said for *kei **runga***. The following *i*, in both cases, is **another** PREPOSITION, which introduces **another**, complete PHRASE.

It is important that there be no confusion here. The correct use of prepositions is one of the most difficult things to learn when taking up another language. This is something that is reiterated in chapter 12, in the section on PREPOSITIONS.

SECTION B: THE PARTICLES AND DETERMINERS

11
The particles: an overview

The PARTICLES in *te reo Māori* are the structural words on which the precise meaning of a phrase or sentence depends. It should not be assumed that the translateable significance of any one particle must be the same in all contexts.

In one context, for instance, *ki te* … may have the significance of 'to the …'; but in another context it may be 'by the …'; and in yet another 'if …'.

Another point is that some PARTICLES are of similar sound (and spelling) to others which have quite different functions.

For instance, each of the sounds *a*, *e* and *i*, as a PARTICLE, has several separate, distinct functions in different contexts; and the word *kei* may, as a PARTICLE, be serving **either** as a PREPOSITION signifying 'at' or as the 'precautionary' VERB PARTICLE ('lest …').

There are probably 'about' 60–65 particles in total in the lexicon of *te reo Māori*. The number is not quite exact because the multiple uses of some words mean that it is not always easy to determine whether or not each separate function of a particular word should be counted as signifying a distinct, separate word in its own right or just another 'function' of a single word. For instance, the particle *me*, Ray Harlow states, may be any one of four different words: two verb particles and two prepositions.

Complete consideration of all the uses of all the particles in *te reo* is beyond the scope of even a much more comprehensive grammar than this one. The aim in the chapters that follow is to provide basic information, with a simple example or two of the use of each particle listed.

Particles may be considered in two broad categories: those that usually **precede** the base word 'nucleus' in a phrase, and those that usually **follow** it. In the case of VERB PARTICLES, however, while most of them precede, two are mentioned here that are found to follow the nucleus. Some 'adverbial' particles may occur in either position.

In the list given here the total count — including three different words for *a*, three for *e*, five for *i*, two for *kei*, two for *mā* and two for *me* — comes to 59. Some variant forms, however, have not been included in this list (for example, *koi/kei* — 'while').

A CHECKLIST OF PARTICLES

1. Particles that precede the nucleus of a phrase
THE ARTICLES
te, ngā, he, a

PREPOSITIONS

ko, me, e ('address') *e* ('by')
i ('connective') *i* ('from')
i ('of') *ā* ('future')
rā ('through', 'by way of') *tō* ('up to')
a, o, nā, nō, mā, mō

LOCATION PREPOSITIONS
ki, kei (or *kai*), *i, hei* (or *hai*)

POSSESSIVE PARTICLES
tā, tō, ā, ō

VERB PARTICLES
e, ka, kua, i, me, kia, kei (or *kai*)
(and possibly *he* should be included here)

ADVERBIAL PARTICLES
tino, ata, mātua, anō (*anō* more often follows the nucleus)

2. Particles that follow the nucleus of a phrase

POSITION PARTICLES
nei, na, ra

DIRECTION PARTICLES
mai, atu, ake, iho

VERB PARTICLES
ana, ai

ASSOCIATIVE PLURAL
mā

anake, anō, hoki, kau, kē, koa, noa, pea, rawa, tonu

Some words that sound identical occur in different places: both *me* and *kei*, for instance, occur **both** as PREPOSITIONS and as VERB PARTICLES. And several words also (for example, *mā, hoki, noa*), are identical in sound and spelling to BASE WORDS of various meanings.

12
Particles that precede the base words in a phrase

THE ARTICLES
te, ngā, he, a

te

('the', singular) *te **whare*** ('the house')

ngā

('the', plural) *ngā **whare*** ('the houses')

he

('a' or 'some') *he **whare*** ('a house'/'houses')

a

This article has no English equivalent. It precedes PERSONAL NOUNS
(but **not** PRONOUNS) when they are the unemphasised SUBJECT of a
sentence:

E ***waiata*** ana   *a **Mere***.

singing   Mary

('Mary is singing.')

but

> *E waiata ana*　　　　*rātou.*
> 　singing　　　　　　they
> ('They are singing.')

It directly precedes PERSONAL NAMES **and** PERSONAL PRONOUNS when following *ki, kei, i* or *hei*:

> *Hōmai*　　　*te waiora*　　*ki a au.*
> 　give　　the water of life　to　me

except that it is **not** used before the variants of *au* such as *ahau* or *awau*:

> *Hōmai*　　　*te waiora*　　　*ki ahau.*

THE PREPOSITIONS
ko me e ('address'), *e* ('by'), *i* ('connective'), *i* ('from'), *i* ('of'), *ā* ('future'), *rā* ('through', 'by way of'), *tō* ('up to'), *a, o, nā, nō, mā, mō*

Any PREPOSITION is **always the first word** in any phrase in which it occurs. This means that there cannot be more than one preposition in any one phrase.

The correct use of prepositions is among the more difficult things to master when learning another language — and *te reo Māori* is no exception here.

One of the reasons for the difficulty is that PREPOSITIONS do not really have a translatable 'meaning' as such. Each has a range of **functions** in the language to which it belongs.

In some contexts a particular preposition in *te reo* may be appropriately translated by a particular preposition in English

— but that does not mean that any one particular translation is appropriate in other contexts.

For two prepositions in particular — *ko* and *i* ('connective') — there are no parallels in English; and for others appropriate translation is extremely variable. In Williams' dictionary 16 possibilities for *ki* are listed, 18 for *i*. The entries in *He Pātaka Kupu* are even more extensive for both words.

ko

There is no English equivalent. It is called the 'focus' PREPOSITION because whatever base word it precedes is the focus of attention in the sentence.

It precedes PERSONAL NOUNS, PERSONAL PRONOUNS or LOCATION NOUNS **directly**:

> *Ko **Hone** tōku matua.*
> ('John (is) my father.')

> *Ko **rātou** ngā **tāngata**.*
> ('They (are) the people.')

> *Ko **Ōamaru** te **tāone**.*
> ('Oamaru (is) the town.')

When the word in focus is a COMMON NOUN some form of DETERMINER will stand between *ko* and the noun:

> *Ko te **kurī** te **hoa** o te **tangata**.*
> ('The dog (is) the friend of the man.')

me

This preposition may be translated by 'with', 'if', 'like', 'as' or 'and' according to context:

Me he **manu rere**		*ahau* …
If a bird flying		I
('If I were a flying bird …')		
te rangi	*me te whenua*	
the heaven	and the earth	

For several other uses of *me* Williams' dictionary or the online *Māori Dictionary* should be consulted.

e ('address')

When addressing people this PREPOSITION is placed before the name (or word of address) if it has no more than one long or two short vowels. There is no real equivalent in English, but sometimes a similar sound of greeting is heard (such as 'Hey!') without the two vowel restriction.

E Rewi!	*E hoa mā!*	But: *Tamahae!*
(Hey) Rewi!	Friends!	Tamahae!

An *e* is used in the same manner, but as a VERB PARTICLE, to issue an instruction or command (see below, under VERB PARTICLES).

e ('by')

A PREPOSITION quite different from the previous *e*, this *e* introduces the 'agent' in passive constructions:

Ka **whakakitea** *mai*	*e ia*	*ki ahau* …
shown	by him	to me …

i ('connective')

There is no equivalent in English for this preposition. It is used to 'connect' a DIRECT OBJECT PHRASE in a sentence with a TRANSITIVE VERB:

Ka patu	*te kōtiro*	*i te paoro.*
hits	the girl	the ball

('The girl hits the ball.')

As can be seen, English has no preposition in this context. Another point is that for some verbs in *te reo*, *ki* rather than *i* is used to connect a direct object (see *ki* below).

i ('from')

As in:

E haere mai ana	*ngā tamariki*	*i te whare.*
coming hither	the children	from the house

('The children are coming from the house.')

i ('of' in LOCATION sentences)

As in:

kei waho	*i te kuaha*
at the outside	of the door

('outside the door')

A further use of *i* is as a LOCATION PREPOSITION (see below).

The PREPOSITION *i* (like *ki*) has many different functions. Eighteen are listed in Williams' dictionary; and there is even greater coverage in *He Pātaka Kupu*.

ā ('future')

This preposition signals a time in the future.

Ka haere	*ia*	*ā te* **Rāhina**.
will go	he	on Monday

('He will go on Monday.')

rā ('through', 'by way of')

As in:

rā roto	*i te pō*
through the inside	of the night

('through the night')

tō ('up to')

As in:

tō te **turi**

up to the knee

POSSESSIVE PREPOSITIONS

a o nā nō mā mō

These six prepositions are considered a distinct group. They really should be regarded as three **pairs** of prepositions — one of each pair featuring the vowel *a* and the other the vowel *o*. All of them, in one way or another, denote 'belonging to'.

This *a/o* differentiation is an interesting feature of *te* **reo Māori** that is present throughout a range of words — including not only the above six POSSESSIVE PREPOSITIONS, but also the pair of POSSESSIVE PARTICLES (which are not prepositions) *tā* and *tō* and their plural forms *ā* and *ō* (see following pages).

Both members of each pair have the same 'meaning'. For

instance, *a* and *o* both have the meaning 'of' (in the sense of 'belonging to'). Which version of any pair — that is, whether the *a* version or the *o* version — is to be used for a given context depends on the nature of the relationship between the 'owner' or 'possessor' and what (or who) 'belongs' to that 'owner'.

Most courses in *te reo* will offer explanations of this system. At this point it will just be noted that the distinction, according to Bruce Biggs (in *LLM*), is between 'dominant' and 'subordinate' forms of ownership. Briefly, this means that things that are portable, things over which the owner has control, and juniors among people are regarded as *a* category possessions, whereas things such as land, houses and seniors belong in the *o* category. Fuller detail is to be found in chapter 14, Notes on the *a* and *o* categories of 'belonging to'.

The example sentences and phrases that follow are aimed at providing specific illustrations of which version of each PREPOSITION is correct in which context.

a/o

These two prepositions both denote 'of' in the sense of 'belonging to':

Ko tēnei	*te pukapuka*	*a* **Mere.**
this	the book	of Mary

('This is Mary's book.')

Ko tēnei	*te whare*	*o* **Mere.**
this	the house	of Mary

('This is Mary's house.')

Such words as 'owner' or 'possessor' might tend to suggest a human being as the possessor of something, but an 'owner', in this context, may equally be something inanimate.

te tuanui	*o te whare*
the roof	of the house

('Parts of things', it could be noted, are considered to be *o* category 'possessions'.)

nā/nō
The prepositions *nā* and *nō* both refer to 'ownership' that has been established in the **past**.

Nā Mere	*tēnei pukapuka.*
belongs to Mary	this book

('This book is **Mary**'s.')

Constructions using *nā* or *nō* thus have some correspondence with what, in English, are sometimes called the ABSOLUTE POSSESSIVES: 'mine', 'yours', 'his', 'hers', 'ours', 'theirs', as well as the form (shown in the above example) of a personal name followed by ''s', emphasised by its 'stand alone' position in a separate phrase.

Either *nā* or *nō* may be placed before any of the PERSONAL PRONOUNS for two people or three or more people (that is, before *tāua, māua, kōrua, rāua, tātou, mātou, koutou* or *rātou* — see chapter 9) to form such an ABSOLUTE POSSESSIVE:

Nō rātou	*tēnei whare.*
theirs	this house

('This house is theirs.')

When the PRONOUN refers to only one person, however, a change takes place. The *nā* or *nō* is **not** placed before *au, koe* or *ia*, but is prefixed to, respectively, *-ku, -u* and *-na*, creating the following set of possessive words (these compound words are shown in bold print):

ONE-PERSON 'ABSOLUTE' POSSESSIVES

1st person ('mine')	*nāku* or *nōku*
2nd person ('yours')	*nāu* or *nōu*
3rd person ('his/hers')	*nāna* or *nōna*

Nāku	*ērā pukapuka.*
mine	those books over there

Nōna	*te whare ra*
his (or hers)	the house over there

The preposition *nā* is also used, both with the PERSONAL PRONOUNS and with personal names, in constructions in which the emphasis is on **who did** an action expressed by a TRANSITIVE ACTION VERB. Further information about this 'actor emphatic' construction is provided in chapter 16.

What might be of interest to note here is that the frequently asked question, *Nō hea   koe?* Although usually taken as asking 'From where you?', it could equally well be asking 'Belong where you?' or 'What is your place of origin?'

mā/mō

The prepositions *mā* and *mō* refer to 'ownership' that is to be established in the **future**.

Mā **Mere**	*tēnei pukapuka.*
for Mary	this book
('This book is for Mary.')	

Mō Mere   *ēnei kakahu.*

for Mary   these clothes

('These clothes are for Mary.')

Like *nā* and *nō*, the PREPOSITIONS *mā* and *mō* form a set of POSSESSIVES with the PERSONAL PRONOUNS and with personal names. Perhaps these might be called 'FUTURE' POSSESSIVES:

Mō rātou   *te whare nei.*

for them   the house here

('This house is for them.')

Mā kōrua   *ngā kai na.*

for you two   the food there

('That food is for you.')

For the ONE PERSON forms (in a similar, parallel manner to *nā* and *nō*) the prepositions *mā* and *mō* are prefixed to *-ku, -u* and *-na*.

ONE-PERSON 'FUTURE' POSSESSIVES

1st person ('for me')	*māku* or *mōku*
2nd person ('for you')	*māu* or *mōu*
3rd person ('for him or her')	*māna* or *mōna*

Māu   *te inu na.*

for you   the drink there

('That drink is for you.')

He inu   *māu?*

a drink   for you?

('Would you like a drink?')

He wai   *mōku* koa.

some water   for me please

Like *nā*, the PREPOSITION *mā* is also used in 'actor emphatic' constructions — in this case emphasising **who will do** an action expressed by a transitive verb (see chapter 16).

Both *mā* and *mō* have a range of other functions. *Mō*, for instance, may mean 'concernng':

*Mō te **aha***   *tēnei?*

concerning the what   this?

('What does this concern?')

LOCATION PREPOSITIONS
ki, kei (or *kai*), *i, hei* (or *hai*)

These four prepositions are called the LOCATION PREPOSITIONS. The **only** BASE WORDS that **directly** follow any of them are LOCATION NOUNS or the variants of *au* ('I'/'me') such as **ahau** and **awau**:

*E **haere** ana*   *a **Hone***   *ki **Ōamaru**.*

going   John   to Oamaru

('John is going to Oamaru.')

Haere *mai*   *ki **konei**.*

come   to this place

('Come here.')

Hōmai   *te **waiora***   *ki **ahau**.*

give   the water of life   to me.

Where the HEAD WORD of the phrase is other than a LOCATION NOUN (or *ahau/awau*) a DETERMINER usually follows the preposition:

Titiro	*ki*	*tēnei pukapuka.*
Look	at	this book.

Hōmai	*te waiora*	*ki a au.*
Give	the water of life	to me.

(The above expression is frequently used as a plea for inspiration when making a speech.)

ki

The preposition *ki* has a wide range of applications. It may refer to actual movement or to some mental or emotional transference from one location to another.

Haere mai	*ki konei.*
come	to this place

('Come here.')

Ka aroha	*au*	*ki a koe.*
love	I	you

('I love you.')

But, besides conveying this sense of 'to' or 'towards', there are several other situations in which *ki* is used.

Williams' dictionary lists 16 different functions, in contexts where appropriate translation may be any of such various English prepositions as 'at', 'by', 'if', 'with' or expressions such as 'according to' or 'by means of'. The entry in *He Pātaka Kupu* has ten sections, each with several various examples of the use of *ki*. The online *Māori Dictionary* (based on *Te Aka*) may be checked (where seven alternative functions are listed).

kei (or *kai*) *i* *hei* (or *hai*)

These three LOCATION PREPOSITIONS (the forms *kai* and *hai* are dialectal variants) are considered here as a group, because each may function as the equivalent of the English 'at':

kei — 'at' in the present

> Kei te **whare**   ia.
>
> (is) at the house   she
>
> (She **is** at the house.')

i — 'at' in the past

> I te **whare**   au.
>
> (was) at the house   I
>
> ('I **was** at the house.')

hei — 'at' in the future

> Hei te **whare**   ia.
>
> (will be) at the house   he
>
> ('He **will be** at the house.')

All three also have several other functions.

Both *kei* and *i* are commonly used with *te* ('the') followed by either an ACTION VERB or STATIVE VERB to form 'continuous tense' VERB PHRASES.

(The construction with *kei te* preceding a verb is an alternative to the construction with *e* preceding a verb and *ana* following it. See VERB PARTICLES below.)

*Kei te **mahi***	*ia.*
(is) at the work	she

('She **is** working.')

*I te **mahi***	*ia.*
(was) at the work	he

('He **was** working.')

*Kei te **pēhea***	*koe?*
(are) at the what condition	you?

('How are you?')

*Kei te **pai***	*ahau.*
(am) at the being good	I

('I'm fine.')

Kei and *i* may also signify 'in the possession of' (in the present and past respectively):

*Kei a **Mere***	*te **pene**.*
(is) at Mary	the pen

('Mary **has** the pen.')

*I a **Mere***	*te **pene**.*
(was) at Mary	the pen

('Mary **had** the pen.')

It should be noted that identical words — *kei* and *i* — are used as VERB PARTICLES (see below).

As well as signifying 'at' in the future, *hei* may denote the purpose for which something is used.

Anei	*he pene*	*hei tuhituhi*	*i te reta.*
Here is	a pen	for the purpose of writing	the letter.

('Here's a pen to write the letter.')

Both *i* and *ki* are used to connect a DIRECT OBJECT in a sentence with a TRANSITIVE ACTION VERB. For **most** TRANSITIVE VERBS this preposition will be *i*, but for others (those sometimes called 'experience verbs') the preposition will be *ki*.

Ka patu	*te kōtiro*	*i te paoro.*
hits	the girl	the ball

('The girl hits the ball.)

Ka mōhio	*ngā tāngata*	*ki ngā tikanga.*
know	the people	the protocol

('The people know the protocol.')

In English, in this situation, there is no preposition.

Ka aroha	*au*	*ki a koe.*
love	I	you

('I love you.')

✕✕✕

As has already been stressed, knowing the correct preposition for all the varied contexts in which they are used (and in some contexts there are alternative options) is probably one of the more difficult aspects of *te reo Māori* for a second-language learner.

The multiple functions of prepositions may be checked in Williams' dictionary, *Te Aka* (or the online *Māori Dictionary*) or the reference grammars of Winifred Bauer or Ray Harlow.

Particularly worth reading is Karena Kelly's already mentioned essay 'Iti te Kupu, Nui te Kōrero'.

Note In English it used to be (and by some still is) regarded as bad grammar to end a phrase with a preposition. For instance, we should ask 'To whom does this belong?' rather 'Who does this belong to?' ('Postposing' a preposition is actually in contradiction to the very name 'preposition'!) In *te reo Māori* prepositions always 'live up to their name': they are always 'preposed'. That is, wherever one occurs it is always the first word in the phrase.

THE POSSESSIVE PARTICLES
tā   *tō*   *ā*   *ō*

The POSSESSIVE PARTICLES *tā* and *tō* are considered to be contractions of the definite article *te* combined with the POSSESSIVE PREPOSITIONS *a* and *o* respectively. Thus, *te … a* produces *tā*, and the single phrase

tā Tamahae tama

has the same meaning as the two phrases

te tama   a Tamahae
the son   of Tamahae

The contraction might be considered comparable, if not exactly parallel, to the contraction of the English 'the son of Tamahae' to just 'Tamahae's son'.
     Similarly, *te … o* produces *tō*, and

tō Tamahae whare ('Tamahae's house')

has the same meaning as

> *te **whare** o **Tamahae*** ('the house of Tamahae')

These particles — *tā* and *tō* — belong within a group of words known as '*t*-class' DETERMINERS, all of which indicate the plural by dropping of the initial *t*. Thus:

*ā **Tamahae tama*** means the same as *ngā **tama** a **Tamahae*** ('the sons of Tamahae' or 'Tamahae's sons'), and *ō **Tamahae whare*** means the same as *ngā **whare** o **Tamahae*** ('the houses of Tamahae' or 'Tamahae's houses').

The particles *tā*, *tō*, *ā* and *ō* combine with the PERSONAL PRONOUNS to form a set of POSSESSIVE DETERMINERS which are used with great frequency and are so basic to the language that learning them should be prioritised. (See chapter 13.)

VERB PARTICLES
e ka kua i me kia kei (or *kai*)
(*he* also should be considered here)

Much of the earlier part of this book is given to explanation of the nature of the two main verb types in *te reo Māori*, which are here called ACTION VERBS and STATIVE VERBS.

All verbs in *te reo Māori* are vastly simpler than they are in English or other European languages. As noted earlier (page 53), verbs in English show changes in form to indicate PERSON and TENSE (for example, 'go', 'goes', 'gone', 'went').

There are **no** such changes in verbs in *te reo Māori*. The form of the BASE WORD remains constant, but may be interpreted in various ways according to the particles that are used in conjunction with it.

What follows below are brief notes on the kinds of information each VERB PARTICLE provides about how the verb is to be interpreted.

e

The particle *e* has several uses as a VERB PARTICLE.

In an instruction:
Similarly to the preposition *e*, used when addressing people (see page 95) *e* is placed before ACTION VERBS that have no more than one long or two short vowels.

E tū! ('Stand up!')   *E noho!* ('Sit down!')

but

Whakarongo! (Listen!)

As future tense:

E karanga   *rātou.*

will call   they

('They will call.')

As imperfect:
When *e* is placed before an ACTION VERB or STATIVE VERB, and paired with *ana* following the verb, a 'continuous' or 'progressive' (past, present or future) tense is produced.

E haere ana   *ia.*

going   he or she

('He or she was, is or will be going.')

E pēhea ana   *koe?*

in what state   you

('How are you?')

E pai ana   *ahau.*

fine   I

('I'm fine.')

In rapid conversation the *e* may sometimes be hardly noticeable: *Pēhea ana koe?* (or even just *Pē ana?*).

ka

The particle *ka* is sometimes called the 'inceptive' because it is used particularly when a new action is beginning, whether it in the past, present or future; as well as when an existing state is being described.

Ka haere   *au.*
will go   I
('I will go.')

Ka pai   *tēnā.*
is good   that
('That's good!')

kua

The particle *kua* signifies the action has been completed, or the state achieved.

Kua haere   *rātou.*
have gone   they
('They have gone.')

Kua oti   *te mahi.*
Has been finished   the work
('The work is finished.')

i

As a VERB PARTICLE, *i* signifies that the action occurred, or the state existed, in the past.

> *I haere   rātou.*
> ('They went.')

kia

The particle *kia* signifies that it is hoped the action will happen or that the state exists.

> *kia haere   rātou*
> ('that they should go')

> *Kia ora   e koe!*
> (I) hope well   you
> ('I hope you are well.')

The expression *Kia ora!* is, of course, the common greeting ('Hello!'). It is also often used on parting, or as an expression of thanks.

Like several other particles, *kia* has multiple functions. Williams' dictionary lists eight, while *He Pātaka Kupu* has six sections, each with several various examples of usage.

me

The VERB PARTICLE *me* signifies that an action should, or ought, be done.

> *Me haere   tātou   ināianei.*
> ought to go   we   now
> ('We should go now.')

The uses of *me*, however, are several, and it's use as a PREPOSITION ('if') tends to merge with its use as a VERB PARTICLE. Ray Harlow's reference grammar offers fuller information.

kei

This is a quite different word to the *kei* used as a location preposition. Directly preceding a verb, this *kei*, sometimes called 'precautionary', carries the sense of 'warning' against something happening.

The following sentence illustrates the use of both *kia* and *kei* as verbal particles.

Kia **tupato**	*kei* **hinga**	*koe*.
Be careful	lest fall	you

('Be careful that you don't fall.')

Many complex variations that are beyond the scope of this elementary grammar occur in VERB sentences. More detailed information is to be found in Bruce Biggs' *LLM*, and in the comprehensive reference grammars of Winifred Bauer and Ray Harlow.

he

The particle *he* is most often regarded as 'the indefinite article' ('a' or 'some') but it would seem a case could be made for considering that it serves also as a VERB PARTICLE.

This certainly appears to be the case when *he* is used preceding an A-type STATIVE VERB (see chapter 6).

He **pai**	*te* **kai** *nei*.
is good	the food here

('This food is good.')

In sentences of this type *he* seems to be usually interchangeable with *ka*.

There are excellent exercises for practicing the construction of sentences like this beginning with *He* in the 'Week Seventeen' chapter of Scotty Morrison's *Māori Made Easy* (see bibliography).

ADVERBIAL PARTICLES

tino   *anō*   *āta*   *mātua*

tino
This particle may be called an 'intensifier'. The English word 'very' is often a good translation.

*tino **pai*** ('very good')

*tino **rangatiratanga*** ('absolute sovereignty')

āta
Commonly preceding an ACTION VERB, *āta*, signifies 'care, deliberation, thoroughness, and so on' (Williams' dictionary).

*Kia āta **haere***	*kei **hinga***	*koe.*
Carefully go	lest fall	you

('Go carefully, lest you fall.')

anō
This particle occurs with great frequency in the 'post-posed' position (i.e. following the nucleus of a phrase) but it also occurs at the beginning of phrases, sometimes signifying 'again', sometimes 'as', 'if' or 'like'.

Anō he **reo tāne,**   *te* **karanga** *mai*   *a* **Hinemoa.**
like a voice male   the call hither   of Hinemoa
('Hinemoa's call seemed like a man's voice.')

(See *LLM* page 141, and also Williams' dictionary.)

mātua

Some confusion surrounds this particle. Although not considered in Bruce Biggs' *Let's Learn Maori*, it is listed in his *English–Maori — Maori–English Dictionary*, (under *maatua* since in Bruce Biggs' books long vowels are marked by doubling the letter) as an adverb meaning 'first'. In Williams' *Dictionary* one meaning is 'first', another 'almost'. In the *English–Maori Dictionary* of H.M. Ngata it is one of the words for 'first'(but without a long vowel). In the online *Māori Dictionary* it is identified as a 'modifier' with two entries: 'first, important, large, must, before others', and 'firstly, first and foremost, primarily'. The example here is from *He Pātaka Kupu*:

Me mātua **hopu**   **koutou** *ki ngā* **tikanga**   *o te* **marae ...**
should first understand   you   the customs   of the marae ...
('You must first understand the customs of the marae...')

The Reed Reference Grammar of Māori (Winifred Bauer *et. al.*) offers (on p. 70) a telling, relevant comment, proposing that *mātua, tino, āta* and *āhua* are 'less clearly particles' and 'must be considered a class of their own on the grounds of their position.'

13
Determiners

In grammar, a DETERMINER, according to the online *Oxford Dictionaries*, is simply 'a word that introduces a noun.'

Thus, in *te reo Māori* the broad group of words that may be called DETERMINERS includes eight particles — that is, the four ARTICLES (*te*, *ngā*, *he* and *a*) and the four POSSESSIVE PARTICLES (*tā*, *tō*, *ā* and *ō*) — as well as the '*t*-class' POSSESSIVE DETERMINERS formed with the use of *tā*, *tō*, *ā* and *ō* (sometimes as 'word-pairs').

A further group of '*t*-class' DETERMINERS are words that are used also as PRONOUNS. An example is the word ***tēnei*** ('this'), which is understood to be formed by joining the POSITION PARTICLE *nei* ('here') to the ARTICLE *te*.

te ***whare*** *nei* / ***tēnei whare***

the house here   this house

Similarly, joining the POSITION PARTICLE *na* ('there, near a person addressed') to the article *te*, produces *tēnā* ('that', near a person addressed).

te ***kūaha*** *na* / ***tēnā kūaha***

the door near you   that door

Joining the POSITION PARTICLE *ra* ('there, yonder') to *te* produces *tērā* ('that, yonder').

te maunga ra / *tērā maunga*

the mountain over there that mountain

(The lengthening of the vowels should be noted in each of the above cases.)

Other '*t*-class' DETERMINERS/PRONOUNS are *tētahi* ('one', 'a certain one') *taua* ('the aforementioned') and the question word *tēhea?* ('Which?').

All '*t*-class' DETERMINERS indicate a **plural** by the dropping of the intitial '*t*'. The words just described may be tabulated as follows.

SINGULAR	PLURAL	
tēnei ('this')	*ēnei* ('these')	(near speaker)
tēnā ('that')	*ēnā* ('those')	(near addressee)
tērā ('that')	*ērā* ('those')	(yonder, over there)
tētahi ('one')	*ētahi* ('some')	
taua ('that')	*aua* ('those')	(mentioned before)
tēhea? ('which?')	*ēhea?* ('which?')	

When one of these words is used as a PRONOUN (a word which may 'stand in place of' a NOUN) it forms a complete NOUN PHRASE.

Ko te whare *o Tamahae* *tēnei*.

the house of Tamahae this

('This is Tamahae's house.')

Ko wai mā *ērā?*

who those over there?

('Who are those people over there?')

Hōmai *ētahi*.

Give me some.

POSSESSIVE DETERMINERS

The other major type of DETERMINER is that of the POSSESSIVE DETERMINERS, which consist of one or other of the POSSESSIVE PARTICLES (*tā, tō, ā, ō*) **paired** with one or other of the PERSONAL PRONOUNS.

tō rātou whare
the belonging to them house
('their house')

tō mātou matua
the belonging to us parent
('our parent')

This 'pairing' of PERSONAL PRONOUNS with POSSESSIVE PARTICLES creates an elaborate yet quite logical and systematic scheme of POSSESSIVE DETERMINERS that occur in most passages of *te reo* with great frequency.

In assigning the 'ownership' of something (or someone) the factors to be taken into account are:

1. Who is the 'owner'? That is, which personal pronoun is to be used?
2. How many things (or people) are 'owned'? One or more than one?
3. Does the relationship between the owner and the possession(s) belong in the *a* or the *o* category?

In the first example given on the previous page, the PERSONAL PRONOUN is *rātou* ('they/them', more than two), there is just one house, and *whare* ('house') is an *o*-category possession.

In the second example the PERSONAL PRONOUN is *mātou* ('we/us', more than two, and not including the person addressed), there is just one parent, and *matua* ('parent') is an *o*-category possession.

Because there are **four** PERSONAL PRONOUNS — *tāua, māua, tātou, mātou* (see chapter 8) — which signify the same as the English 'we/us', and **four** alternatives — *tā, tō, ā* and *ō* — for the POSSESSIVE PARTICLE (see chapter 12), it can be seen that for translating the single English word 'our' there are at least **16** different possibilities in *te reo Māori*!

The process may at first seem complicated — but it is very logical and actually quite easy to understand. Whenever two or more people are the 'owners', all that is involved is choosing the correct POSSESSIVE PARTICLE to place **preceding** the correct PERSONAL PRONOUN.

The DETERMINER in these cases consists of a pair of words. For example, the 'our' of 'our parent' consists of the personal pronoun *mātou* preceded by the possessive particle *tō*: *tō mātou matua*.

When the 'owner' is just one person, however, things are slightly different. (This is one of the few major 'irregularities' in *te reo Māori*.) In the case of the **one-person possessives** the POSSESSIVE PARTICLE (*tā, tō, ā* or *ō*) is **not** placed preceding the PERSONAL PRONOUN. That is, it **does not** precede *au, koe* or *ia*.

Instead (as is also the case with the prepositions *na, no, ma* and *mo* — see chapter 12) the appropriate POSSESSIVE PARTICLE is **prefixed** to -*ku*, -*u* and -*na* respectively. These one-person forms may be tabulated as follows.

ONE-PERSON POSSESSIVE DETERMINERS

	A SINGLE 'POSSESSION'	2 OR MORE 'POSSESSIONS'
1st person ('my')	*tāku* or *tōku*	*āku* or *ōku*
2nd person ('your')	*tāu* or *tōu*	*āu* or *ōu*
3rd person ('his/her')	*tāna* or *tōna*	*āna* or *ōna*

In addition to the words in the above table, which have the options of *a* or *o* forms in each case, there are also six '**neutral**' forms, in which the *a/o* distinction is not made. The six forms are as follows.

taku (for *tāku* or *tōku*)	*aku* (for *āku* or *ōku*)
tō (for *tāu* or *tōu*)	*ō* (for *āu* or *ōu*)
tana (for *tāna* or *tōna*)	*ana* (for *āna* or *ōna*)

As an example, the word *taku* may substitute for either *tāku* or *tōku* — and since the COMMON NOUN *whare* ('house') denotes an *o*-category 'possession', one may say either *tōku whare* or *taku whare* (for 'my house') but *tāku whare* would be incorrect.

These 'neutral' forms now seem to be regarded as the norm in common usage, but they exist **only** for **one-person** possessives. With two or more than two people, making the *a/o* distinction is always required.

tā tāua mahi
the belonging to you and I work
('our work')

> *tō mātou matua*
> the belonging to us parent
> ('our parent')

A further point is that the 'neutral' one-person forms are used **only when preceding a** NOUN. When any of the ONE-PERSON POSSESSIVES stands separately, as the sole base word in a phrase, the 'neutral' form should not be used. The 'correct' (*a* or *o*) form is needed:

> *He pukapuka*   *tāku.*
> a book   belongs to me
> ('I have a book.')

These POSSESSIVE DETERMINERS are sometimes called 'simple possessives', to distinguish them from what are called 'absolute possessives'. This distinction is made in English, between, for example the simple possessive 'my' and the absolute possessive 'mine'. A set of words that can serve as a kind of parallel to the English absolute possessives is formed in *te reo Māori* by the use of the prepositions *nā* and *nō* (see chapter 12).

Like other *t*-class determiners (*tēnei, tētahi, taua* and so on) the POSSESSIVE DETERMINERS indicate a plural of the things (or people) 'owned' by the dropping of the initial '*t*' (as is shown above in the chart of the one-person forms).

Here are some further examples.

ō kōrua kākahu
the belonging to you two clothes
('your clothes')

ā koutou pukapuka
the belonging to you (pl.) books
('your books')

tō rātou whare
the belonging to them house
('their house')

tā tātou mahi
the belonging to all of us task
('our work')

ā tātou mahi
the belonging to all of us tasks
('our work')

Ko Ihowa   *tōku hēpara;*
'The Lord (is) my shepherd;'

Ināianei hoki   *he titiro pōuriuri*   *tā tātou*
Now 'indeed'   a look dark   belongs to us

i roto   *i te whakaata,*
from inside   of the mirror

The adverbial particle *hoki* is an 'intensifier', and the translation 'indeed' an approximation only. In the King James English version of the *Holy Bible* the wording is 'For now we see through a [looking-] glass darkly.')

E tō mātou matua	*i te rangi*	*kia tapu*
Our father	in the heaven	be holy
tōu ingoa,	*kia tae mai*	*tōu rangatiratanga*
your name,	may arrive here	your kingdom

Note A compromise has had to be made with the convention in this book of showing BASE WORDS in bold and PARTICLES in normal typeface. It is hoped it will not be confusing that the words *tēnei*, *tēnā*, *tērā*, *tētahi*, *tēhea?* and *taua* and their plural forms are shown in bold both when they are functioning as DETERMINERS introducing nouns, and when they occupy the 'stand-alone' position (i.e. when they function as PRONOUNS).

tō **Mere** *whare*

the belonging to Mary house

('Mary's house')

14
Notes on the *a* and *o* categories of 'belonging to'

It has been shown in earlier sections of this book, that words in *te reo Māori* that denote 'belonging to' each have two forms, one characterised by the vowel *a* and the other by the vowel *o*. (See for instance the comments on the PREPOSITIONS *nā*, *nō*, *mā* and *mō* in chapter 12, and on the POSSESSIVE DETERMINERS in chapter 13). For some 'belonging to' relationships words with *a* are used, while for others words with *o* are used.

The words involved here are the PREPOSITIONS *a* and *o* (when they mean 'of'), the four POSSESSIVE PARTICLES *tā*, *tō*, *ā* and *ō*, and the four PREPOSITIONS *nā*, *nō*, *mā* and *mō*.

Apart from the availability of the six 'neutral forms' of one-person POSSESSIVE DETERMINERS (see page 119) the category of a given 'belonging to' relationship is embedded in the language. That is, some relationships are defined as '*a* category' and others as '*o* category'.

This is a striking feature of *te reo Māori*, and the words listed are used with such frequency that it is worthwhile taking some time to understand thoroughly what is involved.

A CATEGORY 'BELONGING TO' RELATIONSHIPS

The *a* category 'belonging to' relationships include those where a person who 'belongs' is **junior** to the person to whom she or he is related:

*te **tama***   *a **Hata***

the son   of Hata (or 'Hata's son')

and those where what 'belongs' is **portable**, is **food** (but not drinking water), an **animal** (but not a horse) or **actions** performed or **done to** something or somebody:

*ā **tāua** pene rākau*

the belonging to us two pencils

('our pencils')

*ā **rāua** rīwai*

the belonging to those two potatoes

('their potatoes')

*tā **Mere** ngeru*

the belonging to Mary cat

('Mary's cat')

*Ko te **kōrero***   *tēnei*   *a **Hata:***

the speech   this   of Hata

('This is Hata's speech:')

O CATEGORY 'BELONGING TO' RELATIONSHIPS

The *o* category 'belonging to' relationships include those where a person who 'belongs' is **senior** to the person to whom she or he is related:

te whaea	*o **Mere***
the mother	of Mary
('Mary's mother')	

as well as those where what 'belongs' is obviously **superior to**, or **larger than**, its 'possessor': **land, buildings, houses** and **means of transport** (this why a horse is classified in this category).

te whenua	*o te **iwi***
the land	of the tribe

*tō **Hata** whare*
the belonging to Hata house
('Hata's house')

*Ko **Barney***   *tōna hōiho.*
'Barney (is) his horse.'

Some books on *te reo* provide more extensive and quite specific lists of what types of 'possessions' belong in each category, and most offer helpful suggestions about the principles involved.

In *LLM*, for instance, Bruce Biggs suggests that the distinction 'can best be expressed' by the terms '**dominant possession**', where the 'possessor' is dominant over what is possessed (*a* category) and '**subordinate possession**' where the 'possessor' is subordinate to what is possessed (*o* category).

Ray Harlow's view is much the same: 'The most important single idea … is control. If the possessor … is in a position of dominance and control … then *a*-forms will be used.' (*A Māori Reference Grammar*, p. 158).

Other writers have proposed such distinctions as that to be made between 'alienable' (*a* category) and 'inalienable' (*o* category) possessions.

One simple suggestion for identifying the categories is: *o* for 'over' and *a* (which is pronounced in Māori like the 'u' in the English word 'under') for 'under'.

None of the above, however, provides fully comprehensive guidelines to the correct choice in all cases where the option is either an *a* or an *o* possessive word.

How is one to know, for instance, that the word *ingoa* ('name') or the word *hoa* ('friend') both belong in the *o* category?

Ko wai   tōu ingoa?

('What is your name?')

*Ko **Barney***	*te ingoa*	*o te **hōiho**.*
Barney (is)	the name	of the horse.

In fact, included in the *o* category, besides those that are obviously 'over' or superior, are such 'possessions' as **thoughts, feelings, clothing** and **parts** and **qualities** of things or people.

ōku whakaaro

my thoughts

*te **ora**   o te **tinana***

the well-being   of the body

Also to be taken into account is the fact that some 'possessions' may be considered *a* category in one context but *o* category in another.

An example given by Bruce Biggs in *LLM* is that of ***pukapuka*** ('book'). A book **written by** someone is an *a* category 'possession' of its author, but a book written **about** someone is an *o* category 'possession' of its subject (see *LLM*, Section 13).

Te Pukapuka	*a Raniera*
'The Book	of Daniel' (**by** Daniel)

Te Pukapuka	*o Hopa*
'The Book	of Job' (**about** Job)

With 'belonging to' relationships between people there are also anomalies. The words *tane* and *wahine* are often used for 'husband' and 'wife'. Both of these are *a* category.

te tane	*a Mere*	('Mary's husband')
te wahine	*a Hata*	('Hata's wife')

But a term frequently used for either 'husband' or 'wife' is *hoa rangatira* which is *o* category:

Ko Hurihi *tōku hoa rangatira.*
('Hurihi is my wife.')

Again, in seeming contradiction to a general principle concerning kinship that seniors are marked by *o* and juniors by *a*, it is found that, besides the term *tuakana* ('older sibling') — which is, as would be expected, *o* category — the terms *tuahine* ('sister, older or younger, of a male'), *tungāne* ('brother, older or younger, of a female') and even *taina/teina* ('younger sibling') are commonly treated as *o* category.

WHY DOES THIS DISTINCTION EXIST AT ALL?
It would seem undeniable that the development of this distinction between *a* and *o* categories of 'belonging' as an embedded feature of the language would have not have occurred without there being some practical, cultural purpose for it.

In an article in *The Journal of Polynesian Studies* (Volume 107, 1998, number 4), Agathe Thornton explores the possibility that the distinction might 'express degrees of **tapu**'. (The BEING VERB **tapu** is a word often roughly translated as 'to be sacred' or 'to be under ritual restriction', or, used as a COMMON NOUN, 'sacredness' or 'ritual restriction'.)

Whether or not the original reasoning underlying the *a/o* distinction can be determined, however, does not mean the distinction is without value today.

Indeed, it could be of great value, in terms of (say) transforming social justice and our impact on the environment, if it were agreed by all in our society that land, for instance, or fresh water or even means of transport, could not be 'owned' and privately controlled in the same way as smaller, portable possessions.

15
Particles that follow the base words in a phrase

THE POSITION PARTICLES
nei   *na*   *ra*

nei
The POSITION PARTICLE *nei* signifies 'positioned here' (near the person speaking or writing).

> te **tamaiti** *nei*
> the child here   (or 'this child')

na
The POSITION PARTICLE *na* signifies 'positioned there' (near the person or persons addressed).

> te **kūaha** *na*
> the door there, by you   ('that door, near you')

ra
The POSITION PARTICLE *ra* signifies 'positioned there' (separate from both the person speaking or writing and the person or persons addressed):

*ngā **manu** ra*
the birds yonder   ('those birds over there')

In the above examples the BASE WORDS are all COMMON NOUNS. But the position particles may also occur with VERBS.

*te **whare**   e tū nei*
the house   standing here

In the example above it can be noticed that the *ana* which would normally follow *e **tū*** ... has been dropped, replaced by the *nei*.

While these particles usually follow the nucleus, there are certainly occasions where *nei*, at least, precedes it.

*tāku nei **mahi***
my here work   ('my work here')

Also, it is not quite true that *ra* always means 'separate from both person speaking and the person addressed'. A common greeting, by letter or over the telephone, for instance, is:

Tēnā ra,   koe.
('Greetings to you, yonder.')

The three POSITION PARTICLES — *nei, na* and *ra* — are also very important in forming various compound words, such as the set of DETERMINERS/PRONOUNS ***tēnei, tēnā, tērā*** (see chapter 13) as well as the LOCATION NOUNS ***konei, konā***, and ***korā*** (see chapter 10) and the ACTION VERBS ***pēnei, pēnā, pērā***. The changes in length of the vowels in all cases should be noted.

Although there seems to be no BASE WORD ***pē*** that refers to 'likeness in behaviour', words of the following set of ACTION VERBS are of frequent use.

pēnei (*-tia*)	do like this	
pēnā (*-tia*)	do like that	(associated with addressee)
pērā (*-tia*)	do like that	(associated with elsewhere)

kia pēnei	*tā **koutou** īnoi*
do like this	your prayer

Like many other base words, these words may also be used descriptively.

Hōmai	*he **pene** pēnei.*
Give here	a pen like this

Other compound words include *anei* (signifying 'here is' or 'here are'), *ināianei* ('now') and *ākuanei* ('soon').

Anei	*ōu hū.*
'Here are	your shoes.'

Ināianei *hoki*	*he **titiro** pōuriuri*	*tā **tātou***
Now indeed	a look dark	belongs to us

*i **roto***	*i te **whakaata**,*
from inside	of the mirror

('Now we see only dim reflections in a mirror.')

THE DIRECTION PARTICLES

mai   atu   ake   iho

All four of these particles commonly follow ACTION VERBS, giving a sense of the direction of the action signified by the verb.

They may be approximated in English roughly as:

mai	'towards'
atu	'outwards'
ake	'upwards'
iho	'downwards'

But the functions, particularly of *atu*, *ake* and *iho* are much more diverse than such simple definitions suggest.

mai

The DIRECTION PARTICLE *mai* has almost exactly the same sense as the rather out-of-date English word 'hither'.

E **haere** mai ana   ngā **manuhiri**.
moving hither   the visitors
('The visitors are coming.')

Haere mai   ki **konei.**
move hither   to this place
('Come here.')

Kōrero mai   ki a **au.**
speak hither   to me

atu

The DIRECTION PARTICLE *atu* signals movement in the opposite direction to *mai*, and is often to be translated by 'away' (the English word 'thither' is probably even more out-of-date than 'hither'!).

> *Kei te **haere** atu*   *a **Hone**.*
> Moving away   John
> ('John is going away.')

But *atu* is also frequently used, like *tino* and *rawa*, as an 'intensifier':

> *Tino **pai** rawa atu!*
> very good very very
> ('Absolutely outstanding!')

In Williams' dictionary five different functions of *atu* are listed, but in the online *Māori Dictionary* there are ten!

ake

The DIRECTION PARTICLE *ake* signals movement in an upwards direction.

> *I **piki** ake*   *a **Hata***   *i te **maunga**.*
> climbed up   Hata   the mountain
> ('Hata climbed up the mountain.')

But *ake* may occur just as frequently as a 'comparative'.

> *ka **nui** ake*   *i ngā **otaota**   **katoa***
> (it) becomes bigger than   the herbs   all
> ('it becomes bigger than all other herbs')

Repeated — *ake ake* — the meaning is 'forever' (as found at the end of 'The Lord's Prayer' in the Gospel of Matthew in *Te Paipera Tapu*).
Eight different functions of *ake* are listed in the online Māori Dictionary.

iho

The DIRECTION PARTICLE *iho* signals the opposite direction to *ake*.

... *nō ngā tūpuna*	*tuku iho, tuku iho* ...
... from the ancestors	handed down, handed down ...

The online *Māori Dictionary* provides a list of seven different functions for *iho* (against the five in Williams' dictionary) — and it should be emphasised again that each of the above four particles has a considerable range of functions the details of which are beyond the scope of this grammar.

Also to be emphasised is the frequency with which these four DIRECTION PARTICLES are used. A single page, chosen at random, from Sir George Grey's *Nga Mahi a nga Tupuna* (long vowels are unmarked in this book) was found to contain 24 instances of one or other of these four particles — that is, an average of nearly one instance for every line of text!

Such frequency is explained by Bruce Biggs (*LLM*, p. 74).

> *It is a striking feature of Maori that most actions are given*
> *a directional aspect by the use of one of these particles,*
> *often when the idea of actual movement does not seem at*
> *all appropriate to the verb expressed.*

This comment also makes it clear that an equivalent word may not necessarily be required in translation.

ka kī mai	*ngā tāngata* ...
said	the people
('The people said ...')	

>Ka **mea** atu   a **Māui** ...
>said   Māui
>('Māui said ...')

Interestingly, a cursory scanning of several pages of *Te Paipera Tapu* found these particles to be much less common than in *Nga Mahi a nga Tupuna*. This might suggest that translations into *te reo* (as in *Te Paipera Tapu*) may often be less naturally idiomatic than original Māori writings such as *Nga Mahi a nga Tupuna*, the text of which was derived from writings supplied to George Grey by Māori authors.

homai, *hoatu* and *hoake*

As with the *pē-* of *pēnei*, there is no stand-alone BASE WORD *ho* (not, that is, which signifies 'give'), but the compound ACTION VERBS *homai* ('give hither' or 'give me') and *hoatu* ('give away to someone else') are very common.

>**Homai**   *te rākau whero.*
>Give hither   the stick red
>('Give me the red stick.')

>**Hoatu**   *te rākau whero*   *ki a* **Hata**.
>Give (away)   the stick red   to Hata
>('Give Hata the red stick.')

The compound *hoake* means, variously, 'give, or bring, elsewhere' or 'set out' or 'go on elsewhere').

VERB PARTICLES

ana   *ai*

ana

Almost all VERB PARTICLES precede the verb with which they are associated. One which follows the verb is *ana*, which has been noted as being paired with *e* preceding the verb:

*E **waiata** ana*   *ngā **tamariki**.*

singing   the children

('The children are singing.')

*E **pai** ana*   *ahau.*

good   me

('I'm fine.')

Often though, *ana* follows the verb without the preceding *e*.

Tō ana   *te rā*   *ki te **moe** …*

sets   the sun   to sleep

('The sun goes to rest.')

ai

Although not used exclusively with verbs, *ai* is found following verbs, in the same position as, and replacing, *ana*, when the action or state signified by the verb is habitual or of regular occurrence.

*He **pono***	*e **aru***	*i **ahau***	*te **pai***	*me te **atawhai***
truly	will follow	me	the good	and the mercy

*i ngā **rā** katoa*	*e ora ai*	*ahau,*
in the days all	live	I

('Surely goodness and mercy shall follow me all the days I live.')

Also, where the reason or purpose is given for something being done, *ai* is used — and hence it is found in the formation of the question as to 'why' something is done.

*He **aha** ai?*
('Why?')

*He **aha** koe i **haere** ai?*
('Why did you go?')

In Williams' dictionary eight different functions of *ai* are described; in the online *Māori Dictionary* there are nine. There is a good chapter about *ai* in John Foster's *He Whakamārama*, and excellent explanation of its principal uses online at *Kupu o te Rā* (kupu.maori.nz). Further coverage is to be found in the reference grammars of Winifred Bauer and Ray Harlow.

'ASSOCIATIVE PLURAL'

mā

This particle is used in the following instances.

1. After the names of people, conveying the sense of 'and associated others'.

*ko **Hata** mā*
('Hata and the others with him')

2. After COMMON NOUNS referring to people when addressing more than one person, to ensure a plural sense is conveyed (few common nouns in *te reo* show any difference between singular and plural).

Tēnā	*koutou*	*e hoa mā*!
Greetings to	you	friends!

3. After the PERSONAL PRONOUNS *wai* and *mea* to ensure that the reference is understood as plural.

Ko wai mā	*ēnei?*
Who are	these (people)?

This PARTICLE *mā*, must of course be distinguished from the PREPOSITION *mā* (see page 100–102) as well as from the STATIVE VERB *mā* (meaning 'to be white, clean, pale or pure'); but it is presumably the same word as is used in counting when any of the numbers 1 to 9 are added to 10 or multiples of 10.

tekau mā	*tahi*
ten plus	one ('11')

e rua tekau mā	*whā*
two tens plus	four ('24')

OTHER PARTICLES THAT FOLLOW THE NUCLEUS IN A PHRASE

anake *anō* *hoki* *kau* *kē* *koa* *noa* *pea* *rawa* *tonu*

The ten particles here may be briefly glossed as follows.

anake

The PARTICLE *anake* signifies 'alone' or 'only'.

*ko **ahau** anake*
('I alone' or 'only me')

anō

The PARTICLE *anō* is used with great frequency in a considerable range of different functions (11 listed in Williams' dictionary, 13 in the online *Māori Dictionary*). The significations include that of 'again':

> **Kōrero** *mai anō.*
> speak hither again
> ('Say that again.')

and 'yet':

> **Kāore** *anō.*
> ('Not yet.')

and the reflexive 'self':

> *Ko* **koe** *anō.*
> ('You yourself.')

hoki

This particle is also used frequently, particularly in a great variety of idioms (see the online *Māori Dictionary*). Primary significations include 'also':

> *Kua* **haere** *hoki*   *a* **Hata.**
> has gone also   Hata
> ('Hata has gone also.')

Often *hoki* is used simply to give emphasis, in a manner similar to some uses of the word 'indeed' in English.

kau

Signifying 'alone', 'bare', 'empty', the particle *kau* is, according to Ray Harlow, rare in modern Māori other than in the negatives **karekau** and **horekau**. It does however occur in the current text of *Te Paipera Tapu* (*Kenehi* 1:2).

kāhore	*he āhua*	*o te whenua,*	*i takoto kau;*
was not	a form	of the earth	(it) lay void

('the earth was without form — it lay void;')

kē

The particle *kē* signifies 'different' or 'other than expected'.

Ki *te* **kōrero**	**tētahi**	*i te reo kē* ...
If speaks	someone	in a language different ...

('If any man speaks in an unknown tongue ...')

But it may also signify 'already'.

Kua **haere** kē	*a Rewi.*
Has gone already	Rewi

('Rewi has already gone.')

koa

In Williams' dictionary this PARTICLE is listed as *koā* as well as *koa*, with the sense of (again) 'indeed', 'in fact' or 'however'. Also mentioned is the use of *koa* 'in entreaty' — sometimes simply as a politeness, with the sense of 'please'.

Hōmai koa	*te* **parāoa.**
give hither please	the bread.

('Please pass the bread.')

The expression *ahakoa* has a meaning often taken to be similar to the English 'although'.

Ahakoa	*he iti*	*he pounamu.*
Although	little	greenstone

This well-known saying is usually rendered in English as: 'Although it's little, it's precious.'

noa

There is a BASE WORD — a STATIVE VERB — *noa*, which means 'to be free from ritual restriction' (the opposite in meaning to another STATIVE VERB, *tapu*).

But there is also a PARTICLE *noa*, which carries much the same signification, and which is found in several different idiomatic constructions.

In Williams' dictionary the BASE WORD *noa* is identified as an 'adjective' (which, in the terms used in this book, means a STATIVE VERB) with four different functions; whilst the PARTICLE *noa* is identified as an 'adverb' (and, indeed, it could, here, like most of the particles in this group, be called an ADVERBIAL PARTICLE).

For the PARTICLE *noa*, thirteen different uses are listed, with translations as various as 'without restraint', 'spontaneously', 'gratuitously', 'at random' and 'merely'.

pea

The particle *pea* may follow verbs or nouns, with the signification of 'perhaps' or 'maybe'.

Ka tika pea	*tēnā.*
correct perhaps	that
('Perhaps that's correct.')	

141

Ka mea   *ētahi*   *'He manu pea!'*

said   some   'A bird perhaps'

('Some said, 'Perhaps it's a bird!'')

rawa

The PARTICLE *rawa* is another that is used as an 'intensifier'.

pai ('to be good')

pai rawa ('to be very good')

pai rawa atu (to be very, very good')

If the base word *pai* is also preceded by *tino* we get:

tino pai rawa atu ('to be absolutely marvellous')

tonu

The main signification of *tonu* is 'continuance'. Asked to surrender at the battle of Orākau in 1864, Rewi Maniapoto is said, famously, to have replied:

Ka whawhai tonu   *mātou,*   *Ake! Ake! Ake!*

will fight on   we   Ever! Ever! Ever!

Besides signifying 'continuance', as expressed by such English words as 'on', 'still' and 'always', *tonu* can, like several of the above particles, act as an 'intensifier'.

ināianei ('now')

ināia-tonu-nei ('immediately')

A further point to be made about the PARTICLES in this last group is that some of them, specifically *kau, kē, noa, rawa* and *tonu*

142

(sometimes called the 'manner particles'), are, like other qualifying words, given passive endings when following a verb in the passive. The passive ending added to these PARTICLES is usually *-tia*:

I whāia tonutia   *ngā* **hoariri**   *e* **Rewi.**
were pursued continuously   the enemies   by Rewi

('The enemies were continuously pursued by Rewi.')

Although quite a large amount of space has been given in the last few chapters to the PARTICLES, it should again be emphasised, that this survey is far from comprehensive. Many of the particles have several more functions than have been noted here, and they occur in what can be a rather bewildering array of idiomatic expressions.

Although from some perspectives the PARTICLES might be regarded as the 'minor' words, most of them are used with far greater frequency than even the very common BASE WORDS, and they are in a sense the 'key' to the formation of PHRASES and SENTENCES in *te reo Māori*. Even at an introductory level a reasonable familiarity with at least the principal functions of each is required.

It is also necessary to distinguish certain PARTICLES one from the other, and to distinguish them from certain BASE WORDS of identical spelling. Both *me* and *kei*, for instance, occur as PREPOSITIONS **and** (in a quite different category) as VERB PARTICLES. The PARTICLE *tino*, preceding a base word, has the force of 'very', but the BASE WORD *tino* is a COMMON NOUN meaning 'essentiality'. The PARTICLE *hoki* has a considerable range of functions, but there are also the COMMON NOUN **hoki** (an edible fish, sometimes called 'whiptail') and the ACTION VERB **hoki** ('to return').

The main reason for showing BASE WORDS in bold and PARTICLES in normal print in this book is to make the structure of phrases as visually clear as possible — but this practice also serves to differentiate specifically (for instance) *tino* from **tino**, *hoki* from **hoki**, *noa* from **noa** and *mā* from **mā** (a STATIVE VERB meaning 'to be white' or 'to be clean').

SECTION C: FURTHER POINTS AND OTHER CONSTRUCTIONS

16

Variations in sentence construction

As explained in chapter 3, *te reo Māori* is classified as a VSO language, meaning that the common pattern of a simple VERBAL sentence employs the phrase-sequence:

VERB — SUBJECT — OBJECT

The classification distinguishes VSO languages from languages with other patterns, such as English, which is classified as an SVO language. However, obviously the VSO sequence is far from being the only pattern of a sentence in *te reo Māori*.

For example, a single word instruction or command may be considered a complete sentence.

Whakarongo! ('Listen!')

This is simply a VERB, with no SUBJECT or OBJECT expressed (although they may be implied).

Again, sentences may be formed in *te reo* without using any VERB at all.

Ko Hata	*te rangatira.*
Hata	the chief

('It's Hata who is the chief.' or 'Hata is the chief.')

Although the word ***rangatira*** is classified as a STATIVE VERB ('to be esteemed'), it is here used as a COMMON NOUN ('esteemed person' or 'chief').

With English it is sometimes stressed that a sentence must have a main verb — but often this verb is some part of the verb 'to be' or the verb 'to have'; there are no parallels to either of these verbs in *te reo Māori*.

Sentences without any verb (sometimes called 'equative' sentences) are very common in *te reo*. The meaning in such a sentence is expressed clearly, concisely and adequately without the use of a verb. To provide a fluent English translation of such a sentence it is of course necessary to add a verb (such as the word 'is' in the above example).

Yet again, even in a context where the VSO sequence would be quite appropriate, this pattern is not invariably followed. An example is found on the opening page of the text of *Nga Mahi a nga Tupuna* where the children of Rangi and Papa are discussing whether, in order to make space for themselves, they should kill or just separate their parents. The speech of Tu-mata-uenga takes the form (the marking of long vowels with a macron has been added):

'Āe,	*tātou*	*ka patu*	*i a rāua.'*
Yes,	we	will kill	those two

('Yes, let's kill them.')

Here, the Māori phrases are put in the same order as phrases in English.

tātou	*ka patu*	*i a rāua*
subject	verb	object

But there are numerous variations in sentences in *te reo* where the VSO sequence is not followed. For instance, if the question is asked *Ko wai ....?'* ('Who ... ?') whether in a verbless sentence:

Ko wai	*te rangatira?*
Who	the chief?

('Who is the chief?')

or in a sentence with a verb:

Ko wai	*e haere mai ana?*
Who	moving hither?

('Who is coming?')

or in a sentence with a verb and an object:

Ko wai	*e whāngai ana*	*i ngā kāwhe?*
Who	is feeding	the calves?

a normal response in all cases would be with *Ko* followed by the name or names of the person or persons concerned — and a sentence in full would take the shape:

Ko Rewi	*e whāngai ana*	*i ngā kāwhe.*
subject	verb	object

In such a sentence the emphasis is on the SUBJECT. The SUBJECT, in the terms used by Bruce Biggs, is said to be 'in focus', and is preceded by the FOCUS PARTICLE *ko*. These types of SENTENCES are very common.

'ACTOR EMPHATIC' CONSTRUCTIONS

There is also a further type of construction where, in a SENTENCE with a TRANSITIVE VERB, the emphasis is placed on the 'actor' who has done, or will do, the action expressed by the VERB.

'Actor emphatic' constructions use the POSSESSIVE PREPOSITIONS *nā* for something **already done** (that is, in the past — although it may be in the very recent past) or *mā* for something **to be done** (that is, in the future).

It has been noted (chapter 12) that the primary signification of these PREPOSITIONS is 'belonging to' — so an 'actor emphatic' construction really ascribes 'ownership' of an action to the 'doer' of that action. (Since **actions done** are *a* category possessions, it is the *a* forms of these PREPOSITIONS that are used.)

Thus, in the following 'actor emphatic' sentences the implication is that the action 'belongs to' whoever did it or will do it.

The POSSESSIVES formed with *nā* are used in sentences which emphasise who **did** something (in the past). In this case the VERB PARTICLE is *i*.

Nā Rewi	*i hōroi*	*ngā kakahu.*
Rewi	washed	the clothes
Nāna	*i whāngai*	*te kāwhe.*
He/she	fed	the calf
Nā mātou	*i hanga*	*te whare.*
We	built	the house

The POSSESSIVES formed with *mā* are used in sentences that emphasise who **will do** something (in the future). In this case the VERB PARTICLE is *e*.

Mā Mere	*e hōroi*	*ngā kakahu.*
Mary	will wash	the clothes

Māku	*e kī atu ...*
I	will say ...

Mā tātou	*e hanga*	*te whare.*
We	will build	the house

Bruce Biggs, in *LLM*. has described the 'actor' in this type of sentence as the 'focus constituent' and **not** the subject, and that what is 'acted upon' is the subject (as is the case in PASSIVE SENTENCES).

Although, from the English translations, the above sentences in *te reo Māori* might **seem** to follow the pattern SUBJECT — VERB — OBJECT, it should be noted that there is no PREPOSITION connecting the third PHRASE to the VERB — and that these sentences are in some ways more like PASSIVE constructions, even though the verb is in the ACTIVE form.

Indeed, translation could probably equally well take the passive form:

Nā Rewi	*i hōroi*	*ngā kakahu.*
By Rewi	were washed	the clothes

('The clothes were washed by Rewi.')

Mā tātou	*e hanga*	*te whare.*
By us	will be built	the house

('The house will be built by us.')

17
Negatives

A NEGATIVE, in terms of grammar, is a word, phrase or sentence that expresses (according to the *Concise Oxford Dictionary*) 'denial, prohibition or refusal'.

The simplest form of NEGATIVE in English is the single word 'No' — for which the counterpart in *te reo* is *Kāo*. This is an abbreviation of *kāore* (or *kāhore*), used only to supply a negative answer to a question:

Kua **oti**   *te mahi?*
has become finished   the work?
('Is the work finished?')

Kāo.
('No.')

At least five other words, however, may also be used for 'No': the two words above — *kāore* and *kāhore* — and the words *kāre*, *karekau* and *horekau*.

The word *kaua*, expressing 'prohibition', may also be uttered as a one word negative.

Kaua!
('Don't!')

VERBAL SENTENCES

A verb is only implied in the above use of *kaua*, but *kaua* may also act as a NEGATIVE PHRASE in a negative 'imperative' (or instruction) SENTENCE.

> *Kaua*   *e karanga.*
> ('Don't call.')

Kāore (or its variant *kāhore*) is the word most used to begin negative sentences.

> *Kāore*   *ia*   *e karanga ana.*
> not   he/she   calling
> ('He or she was not, is not or will not be calling.')

Such negative sentences can be seen, as Bruce Biggs has pointed out, as 'transforms' of affirmative sentences.

AFFIRMATIVE

E karanga ana   *ia.*
calling   he/she

NEGATIVE

Kāore   *ia*   *e karanga ana.*
not   he/she   calling

The above example shows that an affirmative sentence in the CONTINUOUS TENSE is transformed into the negative by the placement of a negating word/phrase at the beginning and the exchange in position of the SUBJECT PHRASE and the VERB PHRASE.

An affirmative sentence in the SIMPLE PAST TENSE may be converted to the negative by the same procedure. In the next example, taken from the 'Scheme of a Maori Verb' (sic.) provided at the front of Williams' dictionary, the negating word is *kīhai*.

AFFIRMATIVE

I karanga   *ia.*
called   he/she
('He or she called.')

NEGATIVE

Kīhai   *ia*   *i karanga.*
not   he/she   called
('He or she didn't call.')

Ray Harlow states 'many speakers never use' *kīhai*, and that *kāore* 'can always be used instead'.

Kāore   *ia*   *i karanga.*
not   he/she   called
('He or she didn't call.')

For other tenses of VERB sentences the 'scheme' given on page xxxviii of Williams' dictionary is a useful reference. The exchange in position of the verb phrase with the subject phrase is something which occurs in all the tenses shown, but there are a few other points to be noted.

The PARTICLE *ka*, which has no defined time-signification, may be replaced in the negative by either (according to whichever is appropriate):

a past negative construction (as above):

Kāore (or ***Kāore***)	*ia*	*i karanga.*
not	he/she	called

('He or she didn't call.')

or by a future negative construction (*E **kore** … e …*):

*E **kore***	*ia*	*e karanga.*
not	he/she	will call

('He or she will not call.')

In negating a sentence in the PERFECT TENSE the particle *kua* is replaced by *kia*, and sometimes *anō* ('yet') is added.

*Kua **karanga***	*ia.*
has called	he/she

Kāore (*anō*)	*ia*	*kia **karanga**.*
not (yet)	he/she	has called

('He or she has not (yet) called.')

NEGATING 'ACTOR EMPHATIC' SENTENCES

Affirmative 'actor emphatic' sentences may be negated by placing the negation phrase ***ehara*** at the beginning of the sentence.

*Mā **rātou***	*e horoi*	*ngā **kakahu***
they	will wash	the clothes

Ehara	*mā rātou*	*e horoi*	*ngā **kakahu**.*
not	*they*	*will wash*	*the clothes*

('They will not wash the clothes.')

In his *Māori Made Easy*, however, Scotty Morrison prefers that *ehara* should be accompanied by the idiomatic phrase *i te mea*.

Ehara	*i te mea*	*mā rātou*	*e horoi*	*ngā kakahu.*
not	*the 'case'*	*that they*	*will wash*	*the clothes*

('They will not wash the clothes.')

In fact, **many** of the example sentences given in this book are of just the most basic patterns. Scotty Morrison's *Māori Made Easy* offers a great range of excellent practice exercises with several variations of sentence-patterns.

SENTENCES WITHOUT VERBS

To transform affirmative sentences beginning with either *kei* or *i* the negation phrase is **kāore** (or **kāhore**). *Kei*, however, is not used in verbless negative sentences, and is replaced by *i*.

Kei te whare	*a Rewi.*
at the house	Rewi

('Rewi is at the house.')

Kāore	*a Rewi*	*i te whare.*
not	Rewi	at the house

('Rewi is not (or was not) at the house.')

Affirmative sentences without verbs beginning with *nā*, *nō*, *mā* or *mō* may, in a similar manner to 'actor emphatic' sentences, be converted to the negative by placing **ehara** at the beginning.

Nā Mere	*tērā pukapuka.*
Mary's	that book

('That book belongs to Mary.')

Ehara   *nā Mere*   *tērā pukapuka.*
not   Mary's   that book
('That book does not belong to Mary.')

Nōku   *tēnei pōtae.*
mine   this hat
('This hat belongs to me.')

Ehara   *nōku*   *tēnei pōtae.*
not   mine   this hat
('This hat does not belong to me.')

Affirmative sentences without verbs beginning with *ko* and *he* are also converted into the negative by the use of *ehara*, but other changes are also required, as the following examples show.

Ko Rewi   *te tangata.*
Rewi   the man
('Rewi is the man.')

Ehara   *a Rewi*   *i te tangata.*
not   Rewi   the man
('Rewi is not the man.')

He whero   *te tuanui*   *o taua whare.*
red   the roof   of that house
('The roof of that house is red.)

Ehara   *te tuanui*   *o taua whare*   *i te whero.*
not   the roof   of that house   red
('The roof of that house is not red.')

When the first of the above sentences is converted to the negative by placing *ehara* at the beginning, the *ko* is changed to *a*, and the preposition *i* is introduced to connect the phrase *te **tangata*** to the rest of the sentence.

In the second example this 'connective' *i* is also introduced — and here, since *he* never follows any preposition other than *me*, the *he* is changed to *te*.

Something interesting is to be seen here. In *LLM*, section 25.22, Bruce Biggs has explained that *ehara* and *kāhore* 'can be regarded as verbal phrases' (*e **hara*** and *ka **hore*** respectively) and that,

> *in fact hara 'be wrong' and hore 'be nothing, negative'*
> *are stative verbs used elsewhere in the language. From*
> *this point of view a sentence such as e hara a Hata i te*
> *rangatira is seen to have the structure of a stative verbal*
> *sentence.*

It might be said then, here, in this present book (where *kāore* is used rather than *kāhore*) that when sentences which are without any verb in *te reo*, such as

*Kei te **whare***   *a **Rewi**.*
at the house   Rewi
('Rewi is at the house.')

and

*Ko **Rewi***   *te **tangata**.*
Rewi   the man
('Rewi is the man.')

are converted into the negative they are actually changed into verbal (STATIVE VERB) sentences, and follow the normal VSO pattern of simple verbal sentences, in which the 'object' phrase is connected to the sentence in all cases by a PREPOSITION.

Kāore	*a Rewi*	*i te whare.*
is not (or was not)	Rewi	at the house
(verb)	(subject)	(object)

('Rewi is not, or was not, at the house.')

Ehara	*a Rewi*	*te tangata.*
is not	Rewi	the man
(verb)	(subject)	(object)

('Rewi is not the man.')

Ehara	*a Rewi*	*rāua ko Hata*	*ngā tāngata.*
are not	Rewi	and Hata	the people
(verb)	(subject)		(object)

('Rewi and Hata are not the people.')

It can be seen that in the negative forms of sentences, which in the affirmative are without any verbs, *ehara* and *kāore* (or *kāhore*) could conveniently be viewed as a verbal phrases with translation 'meanings' of 'is not', 'are not', 'was not' and so on.

Could it be suggested, then, that although there may be no equivalent in *te reo Māori* of the English verb 'to be', there are, in *te reo*, STATIVE VERBS that carry something like the meaning of 'to **not** be'?

18
Asking questions

This chapter offers some brief comments about how questions are asked in *te reo Māori*.

Almost any simple sentence in *te reo* may, as in other languages, be turned into a question simply by intonation.

*E **haere** ana*	*rātou*	*ki te **kanikani**.*
going	they	to the dance

('They are going to the dance.')

*E **haere** ana*	*rātou*	*ki te **kanikani**?*
going	they	to the dance?

('Are they going to the dance?')

In fact, intonation alone could equally convert the English translation in the first case into a question (the word order does not absolutely require altering).

'They are going to the dance?'

There are certain words in *te reo*, however, which occur virtually only as questions, and almost any sentence in which any of these words appears is in the form of a question.

These INTERROGATIVES are:

aha?

hea? (or *whea?*) along with *āhea?/āwhea?*

nahea?/nawhea?

pēhea?/pēwhea?

tēhea?/tēwhea? (the alternative versions of these *hea* words are common)

hia?

wai?

aha?

The word *aha?* is an interrogative ACTION VERB (and actually signifies '**do** what?').

> E ***aha*** *ana*   *koe?*
> doing what   you?
> ('What are you doing?')

Note The *kei* (or *kai*) *te* ... version of this sentence is used by some speakers of East Coast dialect to ask about a person's well-being. Thus, *Kei te **aha** koe?* or *Kai te **aha** koe?* may be interpreted as **either** 'What are you doing?' **or** 'How are you?'

As an ACTION VERB, *aha?* can be used passively:

> *Kua **ahatia***   *koe?*
> ('What has been done (to) you?')

Like other ACTION VERBS, *aha?* may also be used as COMMON NOUN.

> *He **aha***   *tērā?*
> a what   that (over there)?
> ('What is that?')

159

When *He aha?* is followed by *ai* (directly or later in a sentence) the question being asked is 'Why …?'

He aha ai?
('Why?')

He aha	*koe*	*i haere ai?*
why	you	went?

('Why did you go?')

hea?/whea?

The word *hea?* (or *whea?*) is the interrogative LOCATION NOUN (see chapter 10) that is used to ask questions about location. It is most commonly translated into English by the word 'where?' Like other LOCATION NOUNS, it may follow LOCATION PREPOSITIONS **directly.**

Kei whea	*aua tamariki?*
at where	those children?

('Where are those children?')

Usually *hea?* /*whea?* will be taken as referring to 'location in space'. But there are several words in which *hea?* /*whea?* is an element — and what is being asked differs in each case.

āhea?/āwhea?

Although the expression *Āhea atu?* is given in Williams' dictionary with the meaning 'How far?', the word *āhea/āwhea?* (which may be written as the phrase *ā hea?/ā whea?*) is usually to be taken as asking about 'location in time' ('when?') in the future.

$$\bar{A}hea \qquad te\ kanikani?$$
$$\text{When (is) the dance?}$$

Āhea	*koe*	*haere mai ai*	*ki te whare?*
When	you	move hither	to the house?

('When are you coming to the house?')

nahea?/nawhea?

The word *nahea?/nawhea?* also asks 'when?' — in this case 'When, in the past?' It is commonly prefixed or preceded by *nō* or *i*.

Nōnahea	*koutou*	*i haere ai*	*ki te whare?*
When	you	went	to the house?

('When did you go to the house?')

The particle *ai*, it can be noted, follows the verb in the last two of the above examples.

pēhea?/pēwhea?

This word is most familiar from the extremely common query:

Kei te pēhea   koe?   or   *E pēhea ana   koe?*

both forms of which (and in either of which the variant *pēwhea?* may be found) ask 'How are you?'

An interrogative ACTION VERB, *pēhea/pēwhea* may also be used descriptively, and in several types of construction. In Ray Harlow's *A Māori Reference Grammar* (pp. 229–30) more detailed information is provided.

tēhea?/tēwhea?
This word is a *t*-class DETERMINER (see chapter 13). As such, it is one of the words the initial *t* of which is dropped for the plural. The plural form is thus *ēhea?/ēwhea?* The question asked is 'which?'.

> Ko *ēhea* *ngā pukapuka pai?*
> which the books good?
> ('Which are the good books?')

hia?
The word *hia?* is classified as a NUMERAL, a sub-class of STATIVE VERBS (see chapter 7). The question E *hia?* asks 'How many?'

> E *hia* *ngā rākau whero?*
> How many the sticks red?
> ('How many red sticks?')

When the question being asked refers to people, the 'human prefix' *toko-* is used in place of the verb particle *e*.

> *Tokohia* *ngā tamariki?*
> How many the children?
> ('How many children?')

wai?
The word *wai?* is the interrogative PERSONAL NOUN. It is most commonly translated by 'who?'

> Ko *wai* mā *ērā tāngata?*
> Who those people?
> ('Who are those people?')

This word *wai?* is used in the common question

Ko wai   tōu ingoa?
your name?
('What is your name?')

The space for translation under the word *wai?* has, in the
above example, been deliberately left empty. This is because it
is sometimes said that in English the question is 'What is your
name?' but in *te reo* the question is 'Who is your name?'

But this is quite wrong — and is a good illustration of the
limitations of translation. The question, in *te reo Māori*, is **not**
'Who is your name?' any more than it is 'What is your name?' It is:

Ko wai   tōu ingoa?

That is, a translation, it needs to be said, does not really provide
the **definition** of a word. Providing definitions of words is one of
the main functions of a monolingual dictionary — and just as an
English dictionary provides definitions of English words, so *He
Pātaka Kupu* provides definitions of Māori words.

The word *wai?* is **not** simply a translation of 'who?' any
more than it is simply a translation of 'what?' In *te reo Māori*
it is a word in its own right. Here, formatted according to the
typographic conventions employed in this book, is the definition
in *He Pātaka Kupu* of the interrogative *wai?*

E pātai ana   *kia **tohua** mai*   *tētahi **tangata**,*
tētahi mea rānei   *e **wakaritea** ana*   *ki te **tangata**.*

The word *wai?* is an interrogative word (*tūpātai*) used in 'asking
a question about the identity of a person, or of something which is
likened to a person.'

But a definition is only realised in practice. If *te reo Māori* is to thrive into the future it must be used in practice continuously.

To the question *Ko **wai** tērā **tangata**?* ('Who is that person?') an answer might be a personal name, or it might be a word describing the occupation, say, or the status, of the person.

> *Ko wai   tērā tangata?*

> *Ko te **kaimahi**   ia.*
> the worker   he/she
> ('He or she is the worker.')

> *Ko te **rangatira**   ia.*
> the chiefly person   he/she
> ('He or she is the chiefly person.')

The STATIVE VERB, *rangatira*, used above as a noun, suggests a fitting note on which to end here. Although it might well be argued that a language could be 'likened to a person', the question here will be *He **aha** ...?* (rather than *Ko **wai** ... ?*)

> *He **aha**   te **reo** nei?*
> *Ko te **reo rangatira**   tēnei!*

Bibliography

In recent years a considerable number of new books relating to te reo Māori have appeared in print, many scholarly papers have been published in academic journals and other publications, and much more material has appeared online. A full bibliography would be extensive indeed. The list here is confined to works specifically mentioned in, or consulted in relation to, this present book.

Dictionaries

Biggs, Bruce, *English–Maori — Maori–English Dictionary*. Auckland University Press, 1990.

Ngata, H.M., *English–Maori Dictionary*. Learning Media, 1993.

Ryan, P.M., *The Raupō Dictionary of Modern Māori*. Raupō, 2012.

Te Taura Whiri i te Reo Māori, *He Pātaka Kupu — te kai a te rangatira*. Raupō, 2008.

Williams, H.W., *A Dictionary of the Maori Language*. 7th edition, GP Books, 1971.

There are several other small dictionaries available in print — but, of course, much more material is available online. The online *Māori Dictionary*, based on John C. Moorfield's print version, *Te Aka*, gives access to a great wealth of free resources offering practice in using the language. *Kupu o te Rā* also provides free online resources — a 'word of the day' sent out by email, and access to much information about te reo.

Grammar books

Bauer, Winifred, with William Parker, Te Kareongawai Evans and Te Aroha Noti Teepa, *The Reed Reference Grammar of Māori*. Reed, 1997.

Biggs, Bruce, *Let's Learn Maori*, Revised edition. Reed, 1993.

Harlow, Ray, *A Māori Reference Grammar*. Pearson, 2001. Note: The book currently in print is a revised edition, published by Huia in 2015.

Bible translation

Te Paipera Tapu, Bible Society New Zealand Inc., 2012. This recent printing of *The Holy Bible* in te reo Māori presents the 1952 text of *Te Paipera Tapu* updated with the introduction of the macron to mark lengthened vowel-sounds.

Other works

Foster, John, *He Whakamārama*, Reed Publishing, 2007.

Higgins, Rawinia, Rewi, Poia, and Olsen-Reeder, Vincent (eds.), *The Value of the Māori Language: Te Hua o te Reo Māori*. Huia, 2014.

Hita, Quinton, *Q's Course in Māori*. HarperCollins, 2001.

Kāretu, T.S. (Tīmoti), *Te Reo Rangatira*. Goverment Printer, 1970.

Kāretu, Tīmoti, and Milroy, Wharehuia, *He Kupu Tuku Iho: Ko te Reo Māori te Tatau ki te Ao*. Auckland University Press, 2018.

Keegan, Peter J. Mention is made of a website, *He Kōrero mō Te reo Māori* in chapter one of this book, but information about Peter Keegan's writings is available on the University of Auckland website.

Kelly, Hēmi, *A Māori Word a Day*. Raupō, 2018.

Morrison, Scotty, *The Raupō Phrasebook of Modern Māori*. Raupō, 2011. Also, *Māori Made Easy*, Raupō, 2015. Since 2015 Scotty Morrison has authored several further books, including four *Maori Made Easy* workbooks (2018) and *Māori at Work* (2019).

Morrison, Scotty, and Morrison, Stacey, *Māori at Home*. Raupō, 2017.

Waititi, Hoani, *Te Rangatahi 1*. Government Printer, 1962. This book was the first of a series of three books on which Beth Ranapia did much editing work. There was also a slightly different version published in two volumes.

Index to main entries for all the particles

Because the particles can be confusing — with several words spelt similarly but being quite distinct in function – this index offers a quick reference to the **main** information in this book relating to each different particle. The aim has been to cover the most frequent uses of each, but the list here is certainly far from complete. (The online *Māori Dictionary*, for instance, lists 14 different uses of the word *i*.)

2 Particles that normally follow base words